dip me in chocolate

AARON **MAREE**

dip me in chocolate

HarperCollins*Publishers*

HarperCollins*Publishers*

First published in Australia in 1998
by HarperCollins*Publishers* Pty Limited
ACN 009 913 517
A member of HarperCollins*Publishers* (Australia) Pty Limited Group
http://www.harpercollins.com.au

HarperCollins*Publishers*
25 Ryde Road, Pymble, Sydney, NSW 2073, Australia
31 View Road, Glenfield, Auckland 10, New Zealand
77–85 Fulham Palace Road, London W6 8JB, United Kingdom
Hazelton Lanes, 55 Avenue Road, Suite 2900, Toronto, Ontario M5R 3L2
and 1995 Markham Road, Scarborough, Ontario M1B 5M8, Canada
10 East 53rd Street, New York NY 10032, USA

National Library Cataloguing-in-Publication data:

Maree, Aaron.
    Dip me in chocolate.
    Includes index.
    ISBN 0 7322 5913 4.
    1. Cookery (Chocolate). 2. Chocolate.
    3. Chocolate industry. I. Title.
641.6374

Cover and internal photography by Brett Odgers
Styling by Janet Mitchell
Internal scraperboard illustrations by Dilys Brecknock
Set in Gill Sans 10/11.5
Produced in Hong Kong by Phoenix Offset on 120gsm Woodfree.

*The publisher has used its best endeavours to ensure that the names and
addresses supplied in this book were correct at the time of going to print*

5 4 3 2 1
01 00 99 98

To those who are mystified by this sensuously dark product, I dedicate this book, in the hope that when the chocolate has been eaten, it will bring the passion closer.

of the world
page 141

chocolate
on the web
page 169

my favourite
chocolatiers
page 173

glossary
page 181

acknowledgments
page 194

index
page 197

As a 21-year-old pastry chef with a passionate interest in chocolate, I looked for a relationship with a chocolate company that would allow me to work in the industry. I found that relationship with the chocolate giant, Cadbury Schweppes of Australia. During my four years with Cadbury Schweppes, I was drawn deeper into the industry than I had ever believed possible — I looked in depth at their production facilities in Australia and England and at the cocoa refining plants of MacRobertsons in Singapore.

During that time, I made thousands of friends. I met a whole range of people — from chocolate professionals to curious consumers — as I travelled the world demonstrating how to work, cook, mould, sculpt and enjoy the flavours of chocolate. No sweeter job could be found and I have been fortunate to work with chocolate and enjoy the pleasure that my work has brought others.

As I now move into a different area in the field of chocolate, I find myself thinking that no other worldly item unifies people quite like chocolate. I have observed that when I perform at any particular event, hushed, fascinated crowds grow stronger by the minute. My audiences are from every age group, every race and every type of person possible. We all find a common ground, a common language — the language of chocolate.

The mystery of chocolate perhaps lies in its dark colour, its aroma, or the fact that we do not know that much about it, except that we love it and are drawn to it regularly. For those who work with chocolate, its mystery perhaps lies in the fact that it is young as far as food products go. Only since 1847 have we had eating chocolate, courtesy of Joseph Fry and Sons. Every year the world of chocolate seems to enter a new realm.

To learn we must have teachers. Through my careers as chef, pastry chef and chocolatier, I have had many teachers, mentors and people from whom I have learnt something of interest. None, however, have ever been like my greatest mentor, Mr David Fell. Without David's awe-inspiring knowledge, technical skills and appreciation of chocolate, I would never have been truly hooked to the chocolate industry.

I am regularly fascinated by the discovery of yet another way that chocolate can be moulded, blended, bound, mixed, modelled, piped, or simply presented. Today, I am more committed than ever to working, to learning, to teaching, and to continuing the art and development of the mysterious love that the world holds for chocolate.

It has been shown as proof
positive that carefully
prepared chocolate is as
healthful a food as it is
pleasant; that it is nourishing
and easily digested [and] that
it is above all helpful to people
who must do a great deal
of mental work.

Brillat-Savarin

melt in your mouth

ice creams,
sauces &
chocolate
drinks

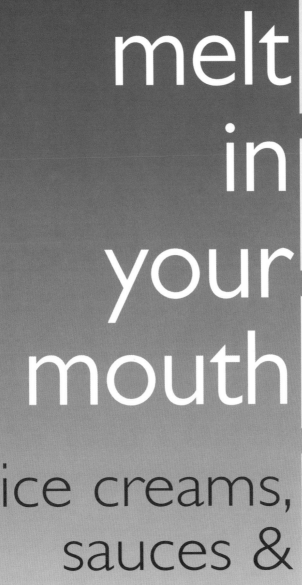

Chocolate Sorbet

2 cups (500 mL, 16 fl oz) water
1¼ cups (310 g, 10 oz) sugar
¾ cup (90 g, 3 oz) cocoa powder
1 vanilla pod
1 tablespoon crème de cacao

Place the water, sugar, cocoa and vanilla pod in a heavy-based saucepan and stir through. Bring to the boil over a medium heat and simmer steadily for 4 minutes, stirring occasionally to ensure the sugar dissolves.

Remove from the heat and take out the vanilla pod. Scrape its seeds back into the liquid.

Cool the mixture to room temperature. Stir through the crème de cacao. Place the chocolate mixture in an ice-cream machine and churn according to the manufacturer's instructions until the mixture is frozen.

Freeze until required. Serve scoops of this sorbet with tart fresh berries such as raspberries or blackberries.

Serves 4–6

Frozen Chocolate Decadence

⅔ cup (150 mL, 5 fl oz) plus 1½ cups (375 mL, 12 fl oz)
double (heavy, thickened) cream

310 g (10 oz) dark (plain or semisweet) chocolate, melted

1 cup (250 mL, 8 fl oz) milk

5 large egg yolks

⅓ cup (90 g, 3 oz) sugar

finely grated zest of 1 orange

2 tablespoons Drambuie

Bring the ⅔ cup (150 mL, 5 fl oz) cream to the boil in a heavy-based saucepan. Remove from the heat and stir in the chocolate. Continue stirring until a thick paste has formed. Set aside to cool.

Bring the milk to the boil in another heavy-based saucepan. Do not allow to scorch. Meanwhile, place the egg yolks, sugar and orange zest in a bowl and whisk until they form a light, creamy mixture.

Whisk the boiled milk into the egg yolk mixture and continue whisking until all ingredients are combined. Allow to cool.

Fold the chocolate mixture into the egg yolk mixture and allow the combined mixture to cool completely.

Lightly whip the 1½ cups (375 mL, 12 fl oz) cream. Fold the cream and Drambuie into the cooled chocolate mixture.

Transfer to a glass baking dish or slab baking pan and freeze overnight. Serve with slices of fresh orange.

Serves 4

How do I know when chocolate is set or usable? When chocolate sets, its high (wet) gloss becomes more subtle and subdued. It is firm to the touch. If you are making curls, you need to intervene halfway through setting, when the chocolate is 'touch firm' (or your fingers no longer leave divots). Scape the curls with a sharp knife or scraper.

3

Frozen Christmas Pudding

⅔ cup (100 g, 3½ oz) sultanas (golden raisins)
⅔ cup (100 g, 3½ oz) chopped raisins
¼ cup (60 mL, 2 fl oz) brandy
2½ cups (625 mL, 1 imp. pint) double (heavy, thickened) cream
¾ cup plus one tablespoon (200 mL, 6½ fl oz)
sweetened condensed milk
150 g (5 oz) dark (plain or semisweet) chocolate, melted
¼ teaspoon ground cinnamon
¼ teaspoon ground nutmeg
¼ teaspoon mixed spice
⅔ cup (100 g, 3½ oz) chopped glacé (candied) cherries
½ cup (60 g, 2 oz) flaked (sliced) almonds, toasted

Soak the sultanas and raisins in the brandy overnight.

Lightly whip the cream. Stand for 15 minutes to bring to room temperature.

Add the sweetened condensed milk, then the chocolate, stirring quickly and thoroughly as you do so. Stir in the remaining ingredients.

Pour the mixture into a plastic or ceramic pudding bowl (about 8-cup [2-litre, 3½-imp. pint] capacity) and freeze for a minimum of 8 hours.

To remove the pudding, place a hot cloth around the outside of the bowl. Serve as a whole pudding or scooped into individual bowls.

Makes about 2 quarts (2 litres, 3¼ imp. pints)

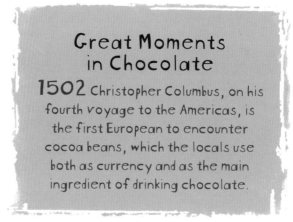

Great Moments in Chocolate

1502 Christopher Columbus, on his fourth voyage to the Americas, is the first European to encounter cocoa beans, which the locals use both as currency and as the main ingredient of drinking chocolate.

White Chocolate and Coffee Ice Cream

1 cup (185 g, 6 oz) sultanas (golden raisins)

½ cup (125 mL, 5 fl oz) brandy

1 level cup (225mL, 7 fl oz) sweetened condensed milk

2½ cups (625 mL, 1 imp. pint) double (heavy, thickened) cream,
lightly whipped into soft peaks

225 g (7 oz) white chocolate, melted

1½ tablespoons instant coffee granules

1 tablespoon hot water

Allow the sultanas to soak in the brandy for 1–2 days.

Pour the sweetened condensed milk into the lightly whipped, and then quickly fold through the white chocolate.

Mix the coffee granules with the hot water until dissolved. Add to the cream mixture.

Fold in the brandy-soaked sultanas. When combined, pour the mixture into a log-shaped container or loaf pan (6- to 7-cup [1½-litre, 2½-imp. pint] capacity).

Freeze overnight before serving in thin slices on a dark chocolate sauce or with a fresh raspberry purée.

Serves 4–8

Moderation is a fatal thing ...
Nothing succeeds like excess.

Oscar Wilde
A Woman of No Importance II

Chocolate Crème Anglaise

1 cup (250 mL, 8 fl oz) milk
1 cup (250 mL, 8 fl oz) double (heavy, thickened) cream
6 large egg yolks
⅓ cup (90g, 3 oz) caster (superfine) sugar
125 g (4 oz) milk chocolate

Bring the milk and cream slowly to the boil in a saucepan over a gentle heat. Whisk the egg yolks and caster sugar in a large bowl until pale and thick. Melt the milk chocolate over a double boiler.

When the milk and cream have boiled, slowly pour over the egg yolk mixture, whisking quickly all the time. When all the hot liquid has been blended, pour back into the saucepan and return to the heat. Stir the liquid slowly with a wooden spoon. Do not allow to boil or the crème anglaise will curdle. Allow the sauce to thicken until it coats the back of the wooden spoon. Remove the pan from the heat.

Slowly pour in the chocolate, whisking until it is completely blended. Strain and serve immediately. Any leftover sauce can be kept in an airtight container with a piece of cling film (plastic wrap) placed on the surface of the sauce to prevent a skin forming. It will keep in the refrigerator for 3–4 days.

Makes about 3 cups (750 mL, 24 fl oz)

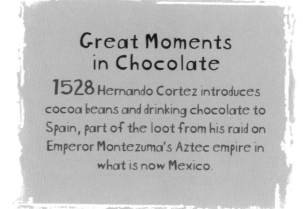

Great Moments in Chocolate

1528 Hernando Cortez introduces cocoa beans and drinking chocolate to Spain, part of the loot from his raid on Emperor Montezuma's Aztec empire in what is now Mexico.

Chocolate Custard

⅔ cup (150 g, 5 oz) caster (superfine) sugar

6 tablespoons cocoa powder, sifted

3 tablespoons cornflour (cornstarch), sifted

2 cups (500 mL, 16 fl oz) milk

1¼ cups (310 mL, 10 fl oz) double (heavy, thickened) cream

1 teaspoon vanilla essence (extract)

2 large eggs

Place all the ingredients into a saucepan and whisk together to remove any lumps.

Gently heat for about 5 minutes, or until the mixture begins to thicken. Continue to stir and increase the heat to allow the mixture to come to the boil.

When boiling, remove from the heat immediately and strain into a serving bowl or into individual bowls.

Makes about 4 cups (1 litre, 1¾ imp. pints)

Hot Chocolate Fudge

60 g (2 oz) unsalted butter

125 g (4 oz) milk chocolate, chopped

¼ cup (60 g, 2 oz) caster (superfine) sugar

½ cup (125 mL, 4 fl oz) double (heavy, thickened) cream

Place the butter and chocolate in the top of a double boiler and stir over a gentle heat until completely melted.

Add the sugar and stir until dissolved, then add the cream and stir again until well combined. Serve warm.

Makes about 1½ cups (375 mL, 12 fl oz)

Quick Chocolate Sauce

2½ cups (625 mL, 1 imp. pint) double (heavy, thickened) cream
250 g (8 oz) dark (plain or semisweet) chocolate, chopped
1½ tablespoons dark rum (optional)

Place all the ingredients in a saucepan and stir over a low heat until the chocolate is melted and all ingredients are combined into a smooth sauce. Serve immediately.

Makes about 3 cups (750 mL, 24 fl oz)

Ultimate Chocolate Sauce

1¼ cups (310 mL, 10 fl oz) water
½ cup (125 g, 4 oz) plus ⅓ cup (90 g, 3 oz) caster (superfine) sugar
60 g (2 oz) dark (plain or semisweet) chocolate
⅓ cup (50 g, 1¾ oz) cocoa powder, sifted
1 tablespoon cornflour (cornstarch), sifted

Slowly bring 1 cup (250 mL, 8 fl oz) of the water, the ½ cup (125 g, 4 oz) caster sugar and the dark chocolate to the boil in a saucepan, stirring continuously.

Mix the remaining ¼ cup (60 mL, 2 fl oz) water with the cocoa, cornflour and ⅓ cup (90 g, 3 oz) caster sugar. Lightly whisk to dissolve any lumps.

When the first mixture has boiled, slowly add the second. Allow to come to the boil again, stirring continuously. Boil for 3 minutes and then remove from the heat.

Serve hot immediately or allow to cool to room temperature before storing in the refrigerator for a cold sauce.

Makes about 2½ cups (625 mL, 1 imp. pint)

White Chocolate Crème Anglaise

6 large egg yolks

2 tablespoons caster (superfine) sugar

1 teaspoon vanilla essence (extract)

1 tablespoon cornflour (cornstarch)

$2\frac{1}{2}$ cups (625 mL, 1 imp. pint) milk

185 g (6 oz) white chocolate, melted

Whisk the egg yolks, caster sugar and vanilla essence until the mixture is very stiff and thick. Fold in the cornflour.

Bring the milk to the boil in a saucepan. Remove from the heat and add the melted chocolate. Stir until the mixture is smooth.

Pour half of the chocolate mixture into the egg yolk mixture and stir until thoroughly combined. Pour this mixture back into the saucepan and stir again to combine well.

Place the saucepan over a medium heat. Stir continuously with a wooden spoon to ensure the mixture does not catch on the base. Allow the sauce to thicken until it coats the back of the wooden spoon.

Remove from the heat, strain and serve immediately. Any leftover sauce can be kept in an airtight container with a piece of cling film (plastic wrap) placed on the surface of the sauce to prevent a skin forming. It will keep in the refrigerator for 3–4 days.

Makes about 3 cups (750 mL, 24 fl oz)

Do I need a marble slab for chocolate work?

No. Glass, ceramic tiles and even metal trays are also suitable for chocolate work. Marble, however, is the optimum surface, as it maintains a constant cool temperature, aiding setting. It does not scratch or stain.

White Chocolate Sauce

60 g (2 oz) unsalted butter
1/2 cup (125 mL, 4 fl oz) double (heavy, thickened) cream
1/2 cup (125 g, 4 oz) caster (superfine) sugar
250 g (8 oz) white chocolate, chopped

Gently heat the butter and cream in a heavy-based saucepan until the butter has melted. Add the sugar and slowly bring the mixture to the boil.

Add the white chocolate and remove the pan from the heat. Stir until the chocolate has melted.

Serve immediately.

Makes about 2 cups (500 mL, 16 fl oz)

Choc Choc Choctail

3 tablespoons crème de cacao
1 tablespoon drinking chocolate
2–3 ice cubes
1 cup (250 mL, 8 fl oz) double (heavy, thickened) cream
3 tablespoons grated dark (plain or semisweet) chocolate

Place all the ingredients except 1 tablespoon of the dark chocolate into an electric blender. Blend on high speed for 1 minute.

Pour into a chilled cocktail glass and sprinkle the top of the drink with the reserved grated dark chocolate.

Serves 1–2

Why does my chocolate melt unevenly?

This problem can have any of a number of causes: a) the chocolate has been overheated, perhaps during a previous melting; b) water, or even condensation from steam, has damaged the chocolate; c) dust has infiltrated the chocolate; or d) the chocolate is old and affected by natural humidity.

Liqueur Lipsmacker

2½ tablespoons Cointreau
1 tablespoon fresh lemon juice
1 tablespoon fresh orange juice
2 tablespoons finely grated white chocolate
2–3 ice cubes
fresh strawberries dipped in white chocolate, to serve

Place all the ingredients into an electric blender and blend on high speed for 1 minute.

Pour the liquid into a chilled cocktail glass. Serve with strawberries dipped in white chocolate.

Serves 1

Mallow Milkshake

1 cup (250 mL, 8 fl oz) milk
4 marshmallows
1 tablespoon soft (light) brown sugar
2 tablespoons finely grated dark (plain or semisweet) chocolate
3 teaspoons drinking chocolate, for dusting

Place all the ingredients into an electric blender and blend on the highest setting for 3 minutes.

Pour into a tumbler and dust the top of the drink lightly with drinking chocolate.

Serves 1

The Ultimate Hot Chocolate

1 cup (250 mL, 8 fl oz) milk
6 marshmallows
1 teaspoon cocoa powder, plus extra for dusting
1 teaspoon drinking chocolate
1 tablespoon cognac

Bring the milk just to the boil. Place three of the marshmallows into the hot milk and stir until they have melted.

Pour half of the boiled milk over the 1 teaspoon cocoa powder and the drinking chocolate, and stir until they are dissolved.

Add the cognac and pour in the other half of the milk mixture.

Pour into a mug and set the other marshmallows on top of the drink. Quickly dust with a little extra cocoa.

Drink while still hot.

Serves 1–2

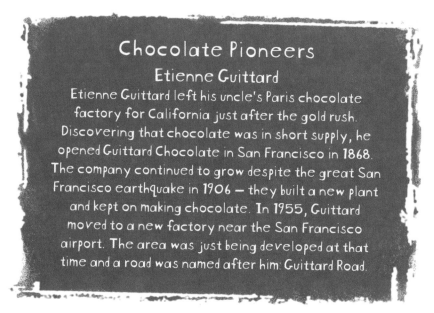

Chocolate Pioneers
Etienne Guittard
Etienne Guittard left his uncle's Paris chocolate factory for California just after the gold rush. Discovering that chocolate was in short supply, he opened Guittard Chocolate in San Francisco in 1868. The company continued to grow despite the great San Francisco earthquake in 1906 — they built a new plant and kept on making chocolate. In 1955, Guittard moved to a new factory near the San Francisco airport. The area was just being developed at that time and a road was named after him: Guittard Road.

Straw Stopper

2 tablespoons strawberry or plain (natural) yoghurt
1 tablespoon drinking chocolate, plus extra for dusting
4–5 whole fresh strawberries, washed and hulled
1 cup (250 mL, 8 fl oz) fresh milk
1 tablespoon chocolate chips

Place all the ingredients except the extra drinking chocolate into an electric blender and blend on high speed for 1 minute.

Pour the liquid into a chilled glass and dust lightly with extra drinking chocolate.

Serves 2

Making Chocolate — from Bean to Bar

Environment

The cocoa tree, a native of the Amazonian rainforest, flourishes in tropical regions around the world. In addition to heat, plantation cocoa trees require the shade, humidity and high rainfall that are typical of their native habitat. West African countries are currently the world's biggest suppliers of cocoa beans, followed closely by South America, Central America and tropical Asia.

Varieties

There are four key varieties of cocoa bean. The Amelonado ('melon-like') bean is the premier variety used in chocolate production. About 40 Amelonado beans, which are purple in colour, cluster inside every pod. The second variety, which accounts for 90 per cent of the world's cocoa production, is the Forastero ('foreign') bean, a high yield, medium-quality product. In contrast, the Criollo ('native') bean is a delicate, subtly flavoured variety which dominated the market in the 18th century. And finally there is the Trinitario bean, a hybrid of the Criollo and Forastero.

Growth

To simulate the conditions of a rainforest, plantation cocoa trees are co-planted with 'cocoa mothers', an array of taller species that provide shelter from wind and rain. The cocoa tree itself can grow to about 15 metres, although it is usually pruned to a height of 7 metres. A tree annually produces about 20–30 ribbed pods in the shape of elongated eggs.

Harvest

The cocoa pods are harvested twice a year. Workers scoop the almond-shaped beans from the white or pale-pink pulp of the pod.

Fermentation

After harvesting, the beans are placed under banana leaves or branches, where they are left to ferment for two to six days. Fermentation breaks down remnants of pulp, prevents germination, neutralises bitterness and causes chemical changes that trigger the development of a cocoa aroma.

Drying

The fermented beans, which are now plump, moist and reddish brown, are moved from the fermenting piles to drying beds in the sun. The dried beans are then bagged and shipped to cocoa processing plants around the world.

Cleaning

On arrival in a manufacturing plant, the cocoa beans are systematically sieved, brushed and vacuumed to remove fibres, twigs, dirt and sand.

Roasting

Like coffee, cocoa beans are roasted in large ovens. This shrinks the bean inside its shell and also intensifies aroma. The beans are roasted differently according to the type of chocolate they are intended to produce.

Winnowing

The shells of the roasted beans are shattered and the beans removed. After being crushed into medium-sized pieces, the beans are sifted and fanned to remove shell fragments from the valuable 'cocoa nibs'.

Blending

After winnowing, the cocoa nibs are crushed into granules, before being weighed and blended into the ratio demanded by the recipe.

Grinding

The blended granules are now ground down on rollers and simultaneously heated, a process that extrudes the butter content of the bean, leaving 'cocoa press cakes' for use as cocoa powder. The liquid content, called 'cocoa liquor', is either shipped directly to chocolate makers or refined under enormous pressures to extract pure cocoa butter, an ivory-coloured waxy substance.

Kneading

The cocoa liquor and butter have by now arrived in the chocolate factory. Here they are kneaded along with sugar, flavourings and powdered or condensed milk, further reducing the particle size of the ingredients.

Rolling

The chocolate mass passes through a series of cylindrical rollers, squeezing it into a paste or 'flake'.

Conching

The flake is warmed and mixed with more cocoa butter, then poured into troughs or round conche machines and stirred for between 8 and 72 hours. Conching creates a smoother texture and enriches flavour. This is one of the most critically important processes in chocolate manufacturing.

Tempering

The chocolate is heated to a specific temperature and then gradually cooled to attain the correct consistency for moulding. Tempering melts the cocoa butter evenly throughout the chocolate so that the cocoa butter achieves perfect crystallisation, guaranteeing the gloss, colour, crispness and 'crack' of the finished product.

Moulding

The tempered chocolate is pumped into moulds, creating solid bars, bars with fillings, individual chocolates, novelties or shaped pieces. After cooling it is wrapped, packed and shipped to the stores where we encounter it for the first time.

Chocolate is not only pleasant
to taste, but it is also a
veritable balm of the mouth,
for the maintaining of all
glands and humours in a state
of good health. Thus it is,
that all who drink it possess
a sweet breath.

Doctor Stephan Blancardi,
Amsterdam, 1705

slice
of
heaven

petits fours,
slices &
cookies

Almond Swirls

2½ cups (310 g, 10 oz) plain (all-purpose) flour, sifted
1 cup (150 g, 5 oz) icing (confectioners') sugar, sifted
1 teaspoon ground cinnamon
150 g (5 oz) unsalted butter
1 large egg yolk
1 tablespoon water

Ganache

½ cup (125 mL, 4 fl oz) double (heavy, thickened) cream
2½ tablespoons Grand Marnier *or* freshly squeezed orange juice
500 g (1 lb) dark (plain or semisweet) chocolate, roughly chopped
⅔ cup (100 g, 3½ oz) whole blanched almonds, toasted

Lightly rub the flour, icing sugar, cinnamon and butter together until the mixture resembles coarse breadcrumbs. Add the egg yolk and the water, and work the mixture into a dough. Wrap in cling film (plastic wrap) and refrigerate for 1 hour.

Preheat the oven to 180°C (350°F). Lightly grease two baking sheets.

Knead the chilled dough lightly until it softens a little. Roll out on a lightly floured surface to a thickness of 2–3 mm (⅛ in). Cut into rounds 2 to 3 cm (¾–1¼ in) in diameter using a fluted cookie cutter.

Place the rounds on the prepared baking sheets. Bake in the oven for 8–12 minutes or until light golden brown. Allow to cool on a wire rack while making the ganache.

To make the ganache, bring the cream and Grand Marnier to the boil in a heavy-based saucepan. When boiling, immediately add the chocolate, then quickly remove the pan from the heat. Stir until well combined.

Allow the chocolate mixture to cool slightly before placing it in the refrigerator. Stir every few minutes until the mixture is thick enough to pipe.

Using a 1 cm (½ in) star nozzle, pipe a neat rosette of the chocolate ganache onto the smooth underside (bottom) of each cookie. Place a toasted almond on top of each rosette, in the centre.

These cookies will keep for up to 5 days if stored in an airtight container in the refrigerator.

Makes 40–50

Chocolate Coffee Truffles

1 kg (2 lb) white chocolate
1 cup (250 mL, 8 fl oz) double (heavy, thickened) cream
90 g (3 oz) unsalted butter
3 tablespoons instant coffee granules
2 cups (310 g, 10 oz) icing (confectioners') sugar, sifted

Roughly chop 625 g (1¼ lb) of the white chocolate. Bring the cream and butter to the boil in a heavy-based saucepan. Whisk the instant coffee into the boiling mixture, then remove from the heat and add the chopped chocolate. Allow to stand for several minutes.

Stir the chocolate mixture until it is smooth and free of lumps. Pour into a bowl, cover with cling film (plastic wrap) and refrigerate for 12 hours.

Using a melon baller dipped in hot water, place balls of the chilled chocolate mixture on a baking sheet lined with cling film. Place the sheet in the freezer for 20 minutes to firm balls.

Melt the remaining 375 g (12 oz) white chocolate. Spread the icing sugar on a clean baking sheet and have the melted chocolate ready in a bowl.

Remove the chocolate balls from the freezer. Dip your fingers in the melted chocolate and roll each chocolate ball in your fingers to coat with chocolate.

Drop each ball in the icing sugar and shake the baking sheet to ensure total coverage. Serve immediately.

These truffles will keep for 3–4 days if stored in an airtight container in the refrigerator. They may need a fresh dusting of icing sugar for presentation.

Makes 36

Great Moments in Chocolate

1671 Praline, a common chocolate centre, is created when an irate chef in the kitchens of the Comte de Plessis-Praslin accidentally tips burnt sugar onto almonds that a boy has spilt onto the floor.

Chocolate Orange Sticks

3 large oranges of a good colour, washed and cleaned
1 cup (250 mL, 8 fl oz) water
1¼ cups (310 g, 10 oz) sugar
225 g (7 oz) dark (plain or semisweet) chocolate, melted
30 g (1 oz) unsalted butter, melted

Using a sharp knife, cut long thin strips of peel from the oranges. Make sure the peel is free of white pith and flesh. Cut the peel into thinner strips.

Place the orange strips in a saucepan of boiling water for 30 seconds. Remove and allow to drain. Discard the boiling water.

Bring the water and sugar slowly to the boil in another saucepan, stirring occasionally until the sugar dissolves. Place the orange strips in the sugar mixture and allow to boil for 8 minutes. (If the sugar mixture is beginning to brown slightly, add another 1 cup (250 mL, 8 fl oz) of water and reboil.) Remove the orange strips and allow to sit on a wire cooling rack for approximately 12 hours or overnight.

Mix the chocolate and butter in a small bowl. Dip each orange strip into the chocolate mixture using a fork. Allow the strips to sit on a sheet of baking parchment until the chocolate has set. If the chocolate will not set at room temperature, place the sheet of orange sticks onto a baking sheet and refrigerate for 30 minutes.

These sticks will keep for up to 2 weeks if stored in an airtight container in the refrigerator.

Makes 15–18

Chocolate Truffles

1/3 cup (90 mL, 3 fl oz) double (heavy, thickened) cream
60 g (2 oz) unsalted butter
250 g (8 oz) dark (plain or semisweet) chocolate, chopped
1½ tablespoons Grand Marnier *or* finely grated zest of 1 orange
drinking chocolate, for dusting

Bring the cream and butter slowly to the boil in a heavy-based saucepan. Add the chocolate and stir until the liquid is smooth, then add the Grand Marnier and stir in well.

Pour the chocolate mixture into a stainless steel bowl and place in the refrigerator. Stir every few minutes until the mixture becomes smooth and thick enough to pipe.

Using a 1½ cm (½ in) star piping nozzle, pipe star or rosette shapes onto a baking sheet lined with baking parchment. When the tray is full, place in the refrigerator and allow the truffles to set hard.

Remove and dust each truffle with the drinking chocolate. Place onto a serving dish and serve immediately. If not serving immediately, place the coated truffles in an airtight container and store in the refrigerator until required.

Makes about 35

What causes grains in my chocolate?

Tiny lumps or grains in chocolate can be annoying if you are piping fine lines or names on cakes. Grains are a sign that the chocolate has been burnt on the base of the melting pot or bowl, and that the burnt particles have been stirred through the mixture. Straining may help, but rarely removes every grain.

Melting and Tempering

Throughout the years that I have worked and demonstrated with chocolate, I have often encountered quizzical looks and nervousness about tempering. Few people have a confident grasp of the process, or understand how it differs from melting.

Melting is in fact the first stage of tempering, and depending on what you wish to do with the chocolate, melting may be the only form of preparation required. As long as the chocolate has never been overheated, or is not too old, it can be melted down time and time again.

Tempering is a process of heating and reheating that maintains the characteristics of any good-quality chocolate that you wish to reset or remould. Chocolate can be kept 'on temper' (as a warm liquid), or re-tempered if required, just as it can be melted or remelted.

How to Melt Chocolate

Begin by grating the chocolate or chopping it into chunks. Place the chocolate in a bowl. Heat water in a pan until it is hot and simmering, then remove from heat. Taking care to protect the chocolate from water or steam, place the bowl in the pan. Allow the chocolate to melt for about 10 minutes, stirring when it becomes soft. The aim is to heat the chocolate to 45°C (113°F), so a specialised thermometer will help here. It is important not to overheat the chocolate or attempt to hurry the process along. When the melting is complete, use the chocolate straight away.

Microwave melting is also possible. Place the grated or broken chocolate into a bowl, leaving it uncovered to prevent condensation. Microwave ovens vary greatly, so you may need to experiment, but short sharp bursts should be fine. Chocolate heated in a microwave does not distort, but instead takes on a shiny appearance, a sign that it is ready to stir. Alternate between microwaving and gently stirring the chocolate until all lumps have dissolved, leaving a smooth, glossy liquid chocolate. Do not remelt microwaved chocolate, as it is likely to crystallise and burn.

How to Temper Chocolate

Tempering is a somewhat complex and delicate process, so if you intend to do much of it you should consider buying a tempering kettle or machine, which uses an automated thermostat and stirrer. If you wish to experiment beforehand, however, start with a modest amount of chocolate (1–2 kg, [2–4 lb]). A thermometer is essential for tempering.

The aim of tempering is to produce a cycle of temperature changes that distributes the cocoa butter throughout the mixture, allowing crystallisation during the cooling process. This results in a good-tasting chocolate with an attractive gloss, colour and crispness. Poor tempering, on the other hand, yields an inferior chocolate that resists setting.

To begin the tempering process, melt the chocolate using one of the methods described opposite. Remove the bowl from the heat source and partially immerse in cold water. Stir the chocolate as it cools, protecting it from water or condensation. Scrape the sides of bowl to prevent lumps and to ensure an even cooling.

When the chocolate has cooled to 26–27°C (79–81°F), it will start to thicken. At this point, reverse the process by placing the bowl in a warm water bath at a temperature of 33–35°C (91–95°F). Mix the chocolate gently but thoroughly to ensure an even temperature. Continue to stir until the mixture reaches a final temperature of 30–31°C (86–88°F).

The tempering is now complete. As you use the chocolate, keep an eye on the temperature of both the mixture and the water, as any changes will cause streaks, dullness or a failure to set. Stir occasionally to ensure that the cocoa butter does not separate. If you need to top up the batch, you may add small pieces of untempered chocolate which have been melted then cooled to 33°C (91°F).

Tempered chocolate coated on dipped centres should set within a few minutes. The ideal temperature for a dessert that is destined for dunking or drowning is 20–24°C (68–75°F). Moulded pieces take slightly longer to set, depending on size. Slow setting indicates unsuccessful tempering. Never refrigerate to hasten setting.

Christmas Puddings

Pudding

½ cup (125 mL, 4 fl oz) double (heavy, thickened) cream

375 g (12 oz) dark (plain or semisweet) chocolate, chopped

2½ tablespoons Grand Marnier *or* freshly squeezed orange juice

Base

1 level cup (100 g, 3½ oz) plain (all-purpose) flour, sifted

1½ tablespoons cocoa powder

3 tablespoons icing (confectioners') sugar

60 g (2 oz) unsalted butter

2 large egg yolks

250 g (8 oz) white chocolate buttons, melted

90 g (3 oz) marzipan, coloured with green food colouring

30 g (1 oz) marzipan, coloured with red food colouring

Preheat the oven to 180°C (350°F).

To make the pudding mixture, bring the cream slowly to the boil in a heavy-based saucepan. Add the dark chocolate and Grand Marnier. Remove from the heat and stir until the mixture becomes thick and smooth. Pour into a baking pan and refrigerate until the mixture becomes very hard.

To make the bases, combine the flour, cocoa powder and icing sugar in a bowl. Rub the butter into the dry ingredients until the mixture resembles fine breadcrumbs. Add the egg yolks and mix thoroughly into a dough. Cover and allow the dough to rest for 5 minutes.

Roll the dough thinly on a lightly floured surface. Cut into rounds using a 3 cm (1¼ in) fluted cookie cutter — about 14 circles. Place on a greased baking sheet and bake in the oven for 10–20 minutes, or until golden brown. Allow the bases to cool on the sheet.

Remove the solidified chocolate mixture from the refrigerator and cut it into wide strips. Cut the strips into 2 cm (¾ in) lengths and roll each length into a ball. Place each ball onto a base circle. (If the chocolate mixture becomes a little too soft to roll, place in the freezer section for several minutes.)

Pipe a little of the white chocolate onto the top of each pudding, allowing it to run slightly down the sides of each one.

Make tiny holly leaves by pinching little pieces of the green marzipan. Place two leaves on top of each pudding, in the centre of the white chocolate. Roll the red marzipan into very tiny balls to make holly berries and place three balls per pudding beside the leaves to form a holly sprig. Chill for 20 minutes before serving. The puddings will keep for up to 1 week if stored in an airtight container in the refrigerator.

Makes about 14

Chocolate Pioneers

Hernando Cortez

The Spanish explorer and brutal soldier who first recognised the potential of the cocoa bean. In 1519, Cortez left Spain for the New World with a fleet of 11 ships containing 500 troops, 100 seamen, 16 horses and an armoury of guns and cannons. Cortez landed at Tabasco, on the east coast of what is now Mexico, remained for a short time to win favour with the natives then pressed on to Tenochtitlan, the capital of the Aztec Empire. The Emperor Montezuma honoured Cortez on his arrival, believing him to be the Aztec God Quetzalcoatl, whom it was thought would one day come from the East as Cortez had done. Among other acts of friendship, Montezuma served Cortez with xocolatl, a ritual drink based on the cocoa bean. Drinking from a gold goblet, the Emperor enjoyed up to 30 daily servings of xocolatl. The gold goblet, and the practice of using cocoa beans as a form of currency, attracted Cortez's avaricious attention. After accepting the hospitality of the Aztecs, the Spaniards murdered Montezuma, slaughtered hundreds of his followers and returned to the coast piled high with booty, including cocoa beans.

During his voyage back to Spain, Cortez (transfixed by the idea of growing 'money' on trees) established cocoa plantations in Trinidad and Haiti. He arrived in Spain not only with cocoa beans, but also with the knowledge and equipment to make drinking chocolate. He is the person most responsible for introducing chocolate to Spain.

Dark Chocolate Fudge

2¼ cups (475 g, 15 oz) caster (superfine) sugar
1¼ cups (310 mL, 10 fl oz) double (heavy, thickened) cream
125 g (4 oz) dark (plain or semisweet) chocolate buttons
1 tablespoon liquid glucose
3 teaspoons butter

Combine all the ingredients in a large, heavy-based saucepan and allow the mixture to dissolve over a gentle heat. Bring slowly to boil, stirring continuously, then allow to boil for 6 minutes.

Remove the pan from the heat and continue stirring until the bubbles subside. Allow the mixture to cool in the pan.

When cool, beat vigorously until the mixture loses its shine. Spread into a foil-lined baking pan (18 cm x 28 cm x 2cm deep) and refrigerate for about 60 minutes until set.

This fudge will last for up to a week if stored in an airtight container in the refrigerator.

Makes 30 squares

Chocolate Pioneers
Macpherson Robertson

In Melbourne in 1880, at the age of 21, Macpherson Robertson founded MacRobertson Confectionery. In 1916, he launched Old Gold Chocolate, and in the 1960s the MacRobertson's firm released the Cherry Ripe bar and an Australian icon, the Freddo Frog.

Kirsch Praline Delights

125 g (4 oz) unsalted butter, softened
310 g (10 oz) dark (plain or semisweet) chocolate, melted
¼ cup (60 mL, 2 fl oz) kirsch
sifted cocoa powder, for dusting

Cream the softened butter in a mixing bowl until almost white and very light.

Beat in the dark chocolate to prevent lumps forming, then mix in the Kirsch. Continue mixing until all the ingredients are combined into a smooth paste.

Using a piping (pastry) bag fitted with a 1 cm (⅜ in) plain round nozzle, pipe small straight shapes about 3 cm (1¼ in) long onto a baking sheet lined with baking parchment. When all the mixture has been piped, place the sheet in the refrigerator for 2 hours to allow the pralines to set hard.

Roll each praline lightly in the cocoa powder. Refrigerate again until ready to serve.

These will last for up to a week if stored in an airtight container in the refrigerator. They may need an extra dusting of cocoa before serving.

Makes 30–36

Marzipan Chocolate

½ cup (125 g, 4 oz) caster (superfine) sugar
¾ cup (125 g, 4 oz) icing (confectioners') sugar, sifted
1½ tablespoons cornflour (cornstarch)
3 tablespoons cocoa powder
2¼ cups (250 g, 8 oz) ground almonds
1 large egg, lightly beaten
375 g (12 oz) dark (plain or semisweet) chocolate buttons, melted
2 cups (225 g, 7 oz) flaked (sliced) almonds, toasted

Mix together the caster sugar, icing sugar, cornflour, cocoa and ground almonds.

Slowly add the lightly beaten egg and work into a pliable dough. If the mixture seems a little dry, add some more egg; if it feels a little moist, add more icing sugar to stiffen the dough.

Divide the dough into four pieces. Roll each piece into a sausage shape about 1 cm (⅜ in) in diameter and cut into 3 cm (1¼ in) lengths.

Dip each of these into the dark chocolate and then immediately roll in the flaked almonds. Place dipped and rolled pieces onto a baking sheet lined with baking parchment. Refrigerate for 20 minutes until the chocolate has hardened.

This chocolate will last for up to a week if stored in an airtight container in the refrigerator.

Makes 48

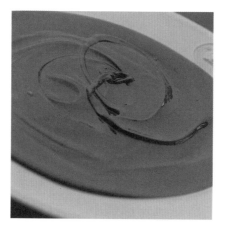

Milk Chocolate Truffles

1 cup (250 mL, 8 fl oz) double (heavy, thickened) cream
90 g (3 oz) unsalted butter, softened
1.3 kg (2 lb 10 oz) milk chocolate
icing (confectioners') sugar, for dusting

Bring the cream and butter to the boil in a heavy-based saucepan. Remove the pan from the heat. Chop 625g (1 1/4 lb) of the chocolate very finely and add to the cream mixture. Allow to stand for several minutes.

Stir until the mixture is smooth and free of lumps. Pour into a bowl, cover with cling film (plastic wrap) and refrigerate for 12 hours.

Using a melon baller dipped in hot water, place balls of the chocolate mixture on a baking sheet lined with cling film. Place the sheet in the freezer for 20 minutes to allow chocolate to firm slightly.

Coarsely grate 300 g (10 oz) of the milk chocolate onto a clean baking sheet. Melt the remaining 375 g (12 oz) chocolate and have ready in a bowl.

Dip your fingers in the melted chocolate and roll each chocolate ball in your fingers to coat with chocolate. Drop each ball into the grated chocolate and shake the baking sheet to ensure total coverage.

Serve immediately or store in an airtight container until ready to use. This chocolate will last for up to a week if stored in the refrigerator.

Makes 36

Rocher Chocolates

2 cups (225 g, 7 oz) slivered (sliced) almonds
¾ cup (125 g, 4 oz) icing (confectioners') sugar
30 mL (1 fl oz) Cointreau *or* other orange liqueur
225 g (7 oz) milk chocolate, melted

Preheat the oven to 180°C (350°F).

Mix the almonds, icing sugar and Cointreau in a small bowl. Stir until the mixture is well combined and slightly moist.

Spread the mixture evenly onto a baking sheet and place in the oven. Using a palette knife, turn the mixture every 3–4 minutes while cooking so that it is evenly coloured.

After about 20 minutes, the icing sugar should lose its powdery look and begin to crystallise around the almonds. Leave the almonds in the oven for a further 10 minutes to brown evenly. Remove the tray from the oven and continue turning the mixture occasionally to allow the almonds to cool.

When cool, break the mixture into bite-size pieces and place in a bowl. Pour over the milk chocolate and stir to ensure the almond mixture is completely coated.

Spoon small amounts of the mixture on to a baking sheet lined with baking parchment. Allow the chocolates to set firm in the refrigerator before serving with coffee. These petits fours will keep for weeks if stored in an airtight container in the refrigerator.

Makes 24

What should I do with leftover melted chocolate?
Allow the chocolate to set at room temperature, then cover it with a lid or plastic wrap until required again.

Grand Marnier
Truffles

½ cup (125 mL, 4 fl oz) single (light) cream
2 tablespoons milk
375 g (12 oz) dark (plain or bittersweet) chocolate
2–3 tablespoons Grand Marnier
¼ cup (30 g, 1 oz) cocoa powder, sifted
2 tablespoons icing (confectioners') sugar, sifted
60 g (2 oz) white chocolate, melted

Bring the cream and milk to the boil in a heavy-based saucepan. Simmer for 3 minutes.

Meanwhile, roughly chop 225 g (7 oz) of the dark chocolate. Add piece by piece to the cream mixture and stir over a low heat until melted. Remove from the heat and stir in the Grand Marnier until the mixture becomes thick and smooth. Pour into a small baking pan and allow to cool slightly before refrigerating for 3–4 hours.

Remove the solidified chocolate mixture from the refrigerator and cut it into wide strips. Shape into walnut-size pieces. (If the chocolate mixture becomes a little too soft to roll, place in the freezer section for several minutes). Set aside.

Sift the cocoa and the icing sugar together in a bowl. Melt the remaining 150 g (5 oz) dark chocolate and have the melted white chocolate ready in another bowl. Roll the chocolate truffles in the cocoa and icing sugar mixture or dip into the melted dark chocolate.

Drizzle with dark or white chocolate, and refrigerate until ready to serve.

These truffles will last for up to a week if stored in an airtight container.

Makes 10–12

What use are
cartridges in battle?
I always carry
chocolate instead.

George Bernard Shaw
Arms and the Man

Whisky Wonder Balls

225 g (7 oz) sponge cake crumbs

3 tablespoons drinking chocolate

1 tablespoon cocoa powder

1 cup (90 g, 3 oz) desiccated (shredded) coconut

¾ cup (90 g, 3 oz) flaked (sliced) almonds, toasted

3 tablespoons Scotch whisky

30 g (1 oz) unsalted butter

2 tablespoons apricot jam

375 g (12 oz) dark (plain or semisweet) chocolate buttons, melted

250 g (8 oz) dark (plain or semisweet) chocolate, grated

Place all the ingredients except the melted and grated chocolate in a bowl. Mix by hand until they come together. (Depending on the moisture of the sponge, the mixture may need more alcohol if it is too dry, or more coconut if it is too wet.)

Take heaped tablespoonfuls of the mixture and roll into balls. Place them onto a baking sheet and refrigerate for 5 minutes.

Have the melted and grated chocolate in separate bowls ready to use. Roll each of the balls by hand in the melted chocolate. Drain and then place directly into the grated chocolate — it is easiest to have a second person on hand to roll the balls to ensure an even covering.

Refrigerate until ready to serve.

These will last for up to a week if stored in an airtight container in the refrigerator.

Makes about 24

Note: For rolling, milk chocolate and white chocolate can be substituted for the grated dark chocolate.

White Chocolate Fudge

2½ cups (500 g, 1 lb) caster (superfine) sugar
1¼ cups (310 g, 10 fl oz) double (heavy, thickened) cream
3 teaspoons unsalted butter
1 tablespoon liquid glucose
225 g (7 oz) white chocolate buttons

Combine the sugar, cream, butter, liquid glucose and 125 g (4 oz) of the white chocolate buttons in a large, heavy-based saucepan. Allow the mixture to dissolve over a gentle heat.

Bring the mixture slowly to the boil, stirring continuously, and boil for 7 minutes or until golden brown in colour.

Remove the pan from the heat and continue stirring the mixture until the bubbles subside. Allow to cool.

When the mixture is lukewarm, beat vigorously until it loses its shine. Spread into a foil-lined baking pan and refrigerate until set.

Melt the remaining 100 g (3 oz) white chocolate buttons. Cut the chocolate fudge into small squares and drizzle with the white chocolate. Refrigerate until ready to serve.

This fudge will last for up to a week if stored in an airtight container in the refrigerator.

Makes 24 squares

Creamy Chocolate Truffles

1¼ cups (405 mL, 13 fl oz) sweetened condensed milk
280 g (9 oz) shortbread cookies, crushed
⅔ cup (60 g, 2 oz) desiccated (shredded) coconut, plus extra for tossing
2 tablespoons cocoa powder

Thoroughly combine all the ingredients except the extra coconut.

Roll the mixture into balls about 3 cm (⅜ in) in diameter and toss in the extra coconut.

Store the truffles in an airtight container in the refrigerator. They will keep for up to 2 weeks.

Makes about 30

Chocolate Pioneers
Milton Snavely Hershey

In 1907, Hershey invented the Hershey Kiss, setting himself on the road to becoming a chocolate tycoon of fabulous wealth. Near his factory in Pennsylvania he established Hershey, a model town for his company's employees, complete with a school, church and other institutions.

Chocolate Brownies

250 g (8 oz) unsalted butter
185 g (6 oz) dark (plain or semisweet) chocolate
100 g (3½ oz) milk chocolate
1 cup (150g, 5 oz) lightly packed soft (light) brown sugar
⅔ cup (150g, 5 oz) caster (superfine) sugar
1½ tablespoons golden syrup or corn syrup
1½ tablespoons honey
3 large eggs
1¼ cups (150 g, 5 oz) plain (all-purpose) flour, sifted
2½ cups (310 g, 10 oz) chopped macadamia nuts
1 cup (90g, 3 oz) desiccated (shredded) coconut
icing (confectioners') sugar, for dusting

Preheat the oven to 150°C (300°F). Grease a 30 x 25 x 3 cm (12 x 10 x ½ in) baking pan and line with baking parchment.

Melt the butter, dark chocolate and milk chocolate in a bowl over a saucepan of boiling water or in the top of a double boiler.

Remove from the heat and stir in the brown sugar, caster sugar, golden syrup and honey. Then stir in the eggs, one at a time, followed by the flour, macadamia nuts and coconut.

Pour the mixture into the prepared pan and bake for 30 minutes or until firm to touch.

Allow to cool in the pan and dust with icing sugar before cutting into squares to serve.

Makes 25–30 portions

Great Moments in Chocolate

1745 Jean Etienne Liotard paints 'La Belle Chocolatiere', a portrait of a Viennese chocolate house waitress who had married an Austrian nobleman. In 1860, Baker's Chocolate adopts the picture as a trademark.

Chocolate Caramel Slice

Base
125 g (4 oz) butter
1/2 cup (125 g, 4 oz) sugar
1 large egg
1 tablespoon golden syrup *or* corn syrup
1 tablespoon cocoa powder
1 1/2 cups (185 g, 6 oz) plain (all-purpose) flour

Filling
1 2/3 cups (400 mL, 13 fl oz) sweetened condensed milk
30 g (1 oz) butter
2 tablespoons golden syrup *or* corn syrup

Topping
125 g (4 oz) dark (plain or semisweet) chocolate
30 g (1 oz) butter

Preheat the oven to 180°C (350°F). Grease a 25 x 18 cm (10 x 7 in) slab pan.

To make the base, cream the butter and sugar until light and fluffy. Add the egg and mix well. Now add the golden syrup. Mix in the cocoa and flour until thoroughly combined.

Spread the mixture over the bottom of the prepared pan. Bake in the oven for 15 minutes.

To make the filling, combine the ingredients in a saucepan and slowly bring to the boil. Simmer for 15 minutes or until a light golden colour. Pour the filling over the cooked base and bake for a further 10 minutes. Allow to cool in the pan.

To make the topping, melt the butter and chocolate in a saucepan or microwave. Blend and pour over the top of the slice. Allow to set at room temperature.

Cut into squares, chill and serve.

Makes 24

Chocolate
Coconut Slice

185 g (6 oz) unsalted butter
2¼ cups (375 g, 12 oz) soft (light) brown sugar
1¾ cups (225 g, 7 oz) plain (all-purpose) flour
2 tablespoons raspberry jam
3 large eggs
1 teaspoon baking powder, sifted
1 tablespoon cocoa powder
1 cup (90 g, 3 oz) desiccated (shredded) coconut
1½ cups (150 g, 5 oz) chopped walnuts
icing (confectioners') sugar, for dusting

Preheat the oven to 180°C (350°F). Grease and line a 28 x 18 x 2 cm (11 x 7 x ¾ in) baking pan.

Cream the butter and ¾ cup (125 g, 4 oz) of the brown sugar until light and pale.

Add 1½ cups (185 g, 6 oz) of the flour and mix to a crumbly texture. Press the mixture into the prepared pan.

Bake in the oven for 25 minutes or until golden brown. Remove from the oven and allow to cool. Do not turn the oven off.

When the base is cool, spread it thinly with the raspberry jam.

Beat the eggs until they are light and fluffy. Add the remaining 1½ cups (250 g, 8 oz) brown sugar and ¼ cup (30 g, 1 oz) flour, and the baking powder and cocoa.

Stir in the coconut and walnuts. Spread the mixture over the jam-covered base and bake for a further 30–35 minutes.

Cut into portions while still warm and dust with icing sugar. Allow to cool before cutting into slices and serving.

Makes 20–24

Chocolate Pioneers
Henri Nestlé
Inventor, in the 1860s, of condensed milk, the product that led to the development of milk chocolate. The company Henri Nestlé founded has grown into an immense global enterprise.

Hedgehog

225 g (7 oz) butter

1 cup (225 g, 7 oz) caster (superfine) sugar

²⁄₃ cup (60 g, 2 oz) desiccated (shredded) coconut

¹⁄₂ cup (60 g, 2 oz) cocoa powder, sifted

3 large eggs, lightly beaten

400 g (13 oz) sweet shortbread cookies, crushed

Chocolate Icing

1 cup (185 g, 6 oz) icing (confectioners') sugar

3 tablespoons cocoa powder

warm water

100 g (3¹⁄₂ oz) chocolate chips

Lightly grease a 28 x 18 x 2 cm (11 x 7 x ³⁄₄ in) baking pan.

Melt the butter, sugar, coconut and cocoa in a saucepan over a low heat. Bring slowly to the boil and boil for 2 minutes.

Remove from the heat and quickly whisk in the eggs. Pour over the crushed cookies and stir with a wooden spoon until all ingredients are well combined.

Pour the mixture into the prepared pan and chill in the refrigerator.

To make the chocolate icing, sift the icing sugar and cocoa powder into a bowl. Add warm water gradually — just enough to make a paste of spreadable consistency.

When the base is cool, spread with the chocolate icing. Sprinkle the chocolate chips over the top and cut into finger-sized portions.

Makes 24–27

Chocolate Pioneers

Philippe Suchard

Born in 1797, Suchard's name lives on today as a brand name on many of the world's finest chocolate products. In 1815, he began work as an apprentice confectioner and, in 1824, he left Switzerland to the United States. When he returned in 1826, he went into the confectionery business himself, in Neuchatel.

Rocky Road Slice

Base

1 level cup (100 g, 3½ oz) plain (all-purpose) flour
1½ tablespoons cocoa powder
3 tablespoons icing (confectioners') sugar
60 g (2 oz) unsalted butter
1 large egg

Topping

250 g (8 oz) dark (plain or semisweet) chocolate, melted
60 g (2 oz) unsalted butter, melted
45 g (1½ oz) copha (white coconut fat or vegetable shortening), melted
250 g (8 oz) marshmallows, cut into small pieces
75 g (2½ oz) macadamia nuts, chopped
45 g (1½ oz) whole glacé (candied) cherries

Preheat the oven to 180°C (350°F). Line a 28 x 18 x 2 cm (11 x 7 x ¾ in) baking pan with baking parchment.

To make the base, sift the flour, cocoa powder and icing sugar into a bowl. Lightly rub in the butter until the mixture resembles fresh breadcrumbs.

Add the egg and mix to a dough. Press the dough into the prepared pan. Bake in the oven for 10 minutes. Allow to cool.

To make the topping, mix the chocolate, butter and copha together. Place the marshmallows, macadamias and cherries in a bowl and pour the chocolate mixture over the top.

Work quickly to combine all the ingredients and then pour onto the cooled base. Spread evenly, then allow to set in the refrigerator before cutting into squares with a hot knife. Portions can then be stored in an airtight container in the refrigerator.

Makes 16

Triple Chocolate Brownies

125 g (4 oz) butter, roughly chopped
225 g (7 oz) dark (plain or semisweet) chocolate, roughly chopped
2 large eggs, lightly beaten
$\frac{1}{2}$ cup (125 g, 4 oz) caster (superfine) sugar
1$\frac{1}{4}$ cups (150 g, 5 oz) plain (all-purpose) flour, sifted
150 g (5 oz) white chocolate buttons
100 g (3$\frac{1}{2}$ oz) milk chocolate, chopped

Preheat the oven to 160°C (325°F). Lightly grease a deep 20 cm (8 in) square cake pan and line with baking parchment.

Melt the butter and dark chocolate in a saucepan over a low heat.

Remove from the heat, then stir in the eggs and caster sugar. Add the flour and combine. Gently fold through the white and milk chocolates.

Pour the mixture into the prepared pan and bake in the oven for 35 minutes or until firm to touch in the centre.

Allow to cool in the pan before turning out and cutting into squares.

Makes 25

Chocolate Pioneers

Guy and Liliane Foubert

The founders of the the 'Guy' — 'Lian' (Guylian) Belgian chocolate company have been producing their original creations since the 1960s. Their chocolate seashells of multi-coloured chocolate and fine praline filling are their most noted product.

The Ultimate Tollhouse Slice

Base

1 level cup (100 g, 3½ oz) plain (all-purpose) flour
1½ tablespoons cocoa powder
3 tablespoons icing (confectioners') sugar
60 g (2 oz) unsalted butter
1 large egg white

Topping

1⅔ cups (400 mL, 13 fl oz) sweetened condensed milk
1¼ cups (60 g, 2 oz) shredded (flaked) coconut
½ cup (60 g, 2 oz) slivered (sliced) almonds
100 g (3½ oz) white chocolate buttons
100 g (3½ oz) chocolate chips

Preheat the oven to 160°C (325°F). Grease a 28 x 18 x 2 cm (11 x 7 x ¾ in) baking pan and line with baking parchment.

To make the base, sift the flour, cocoa powder and icing sugar into a bowl. Lightly rub in the butter until the mixture resembles fine breadcrumbs.

Add egg white and mix thoroughly. Turn the dough onto a lightly floured surface and knead lightly.

Press the dough into the prepared pan. Bake for 10 minutes or until golden brown, then remove from the oven and set aside to cool. Reduce the oven temperature to 140°C (275°F).

When the base is cool, spread half of the sweetened condensed milk over the top, then sprinkle with the coconut, almonds, white chocolate buttons and chocolate chips. Pour over the remaining sweetened condensed milk.

Bake in the oven for a further 30 minutes. Allow to cool for 20 minutes before refrigerating for 1 hour. Cut into portions to serve.

Makes 24

Afghans

225 g (7 oz) unsalted butter, softened
¾ cup (125 g, 4 oz) firmly packed soft (light) brown sugar
1 tablespoon clear honey
1 large egg
2¼ cups (280 g, 9 oz) plain (all-purpose) flour
3 tablespoons cocoa powder
2 teaspoons baking powder (double-acting)
⅔ cup (60 g, 2 oz) desiccated (shredded) coconut
1 teaspoon vanilla essence (extract)
2½ cups (75 g, 2½ oz) cornflakes

Icing

¾ cup (125 g, 4 oz) icing (confectioners') sugar
2 tablespoons drinking chocolate
3–4 teaspoons hot water
chocolate chips

Preheat the oven to 180°C (350°F). Line two baking sheets with parchment paper.

Cream the butter and sugar until light and fluffy. Add the honey and egg, and combine well.

Sift the flour, cocoa powder and baking powder into the mixture, then add the coconut and vanilla essence. Mix thoroughly. Lastly, add the cornflakes and mix lightly, taking care not to break up the cornflakes.

Place heaped tablespoons of the mixture onto the baking sheets, leaving room between each cookie for spreading.

Bake in the oven for 8–10 minutes, until golden brown. Slide the cookies off the baking sheets and onto a wire cooling rack.

To make the icing, sift together the icing sugar and drinking chocolate. Slowly add the water until a thick paste has formed. Use immediately.

Drizzle 1 teaspoon of the chocolate icing over the top of each cookie. Before the icing sets, sprinkle each cookie liberally with chocolate chips.

Makes 24–30

Amaree Cookies

185 g (6 oz) unsalted butter, softened
1 cup (185 g, 6 oz) soft (light) brown sugar
1/3 cup (90 mL, 3 fl oz) golden syrup or corn syrup
1 large egg
2 cups (250 g, 8 oz) plain (all-purpose) flour
2 teaspoons baking powder
2 tablespoons cocoa powder
2 teaspoons ground cinnamon
raw or demerara sugar
225 g (7 oz) dark chocolate, melted
225 g (7 oz) sesame seeds, toasted

Cream the butter, sugar and golden syrup until light and fluffy. Add the egg and mix until combined.

Sift the flour, baking powder, cocoa powder and cinnamon together, then add in two batches to the creamed mixture. Mix thoroughly.

Form the mixture into a ball. Cover with cling film (plastic wrap) and refrigerate for 45 minutes.

Preheat the oven to 180°C (250°F). Line baking sheets with baking parchment.

Remove the dough from the refrigerator. Take walnut-size portions and roll into balls. Dip half of each ball into the raw sugar and place on the prepared sheet. Allow at least 5 cm (2 in) between each cookie for spreading.

Bake in the oven for 10–12 minutes, and allow to cool slightly on the baking sheet before sliding onto a wire rack.

When the cookies are cool, lightly dip the undersides or bottoms in the dark chocolate, and then in the sesame seeds. Place on a baking sheet and leave in the refrigerator for 20 minutes or until set.

Makes 24

Chocolate Pioneers
Jean Neuhaus

In 1857, Jean Neuhaus left his native Switzerland to settle in Belgium with his brother-in-law, a chemist. They opened a pharmacy and confectionery shop, for which Jean Neuhaus made cough drops, liquorice to cure heartburn and some bars of dark chocolate. Over next 50 years, successive generations shifted the focus to confections and today Neuhaus stores can be found around the globe.

Chequerboard Cookies

White Dough

1¾ cups (225 g, 7 oz) plain (all-purpose) flour

½ cup (90 g, 3 oz) icing (confectioners') sugar

150 g (5 oz) unsalted butter

1 large egg, separated

Chocolate Dough

1½ cups (185 g, 6 oz) plain (all-purpose) flour

½ cup (90 g, 3 oz) icing (confectioners') sugar

3 tablespoons cocoa powder

150 g (5 oz) unsalted butter

2 large egg yolks

egg white

To make the white dough, sift the flour and icing sugar together into a bowl. Lightly rub the butter into the dry ingredients. Add the egg and continue mixing until a dough is formed. Set aside.

To make the chocolate dough, sift the flour, icing sugar and cocoa together into a bowl. Lightly rub the butter into the dry ingredients. Add the egg yolks and continue mixing until a dough is formed.

Wrap each ball of dough in cling film (plastic wrap) and refrigerate for 1 hour. Remove and knead each ball of dough lightly until it is soft enough to roll.

Roll both doughs into squares about 1 cm (⅜ in) thick on a lightly floured surface. Cut four strips 1 cm (⅜ in) wide from the chocolate dough and five strips 1 cm (⅜ in) wide from the white dough.

Knead together any scrap pastry from the doughs into a ball. Roll the scrap pastry — it should now be milk chocolate in colour — so that it is 2–3 mm (⅛ in) thick, the same length as the white and chocolate strips, and as wide as possible. Lightly brush the top with egg white.

Place the strips of white and chocolate side by side lengthwise and alternately — a strip of white pastry, a strip of chocolate pastry, a strip of white pastry. Brush lightly with egg white.

Repeat the process on top of this layer, but starting with a strip of chocolate pastry so that a chocolate strip is placed on top of a white strip and vice versa. Brush this layer with egg white.

Make a third layer repeating the process, again alternating the colours. Brush this layer with egg white.

Lightly brush egg white around the sides of the layers. Lay the milk chocolate pastry flat over the top, pressing the outer edges of the milk chocolate pastry around the chequerboard layers so that they are completely covered by the milk chocolate pastry. Trim away any excess milk chocolate pastry. Place in the refrigerator for 1 hour.

Preheat the oven to 180°C (350°F). Line two baking sheets with baking parchment.

Remove the chequerboard dough from the refrigerator and cut across the dough into 5 mm (¼ in) thicknesses. Place the slices flat on the prepared baking sheet so that the chequerboard design is facing upwards. Bake in the oven for 8–10 minutes, or until the white pieces are lightly browning around the edge.

Remove from the oven and cool slightly before eating fresh.

These cookies will keep for up to a week if stored in an airtight container.

Makes 24

Should I ever use compound chocolate?

Compound chocolate is criticised in many cooking magazines, where often only the most fashionable (and expensive) chocolate is recommended, but while it is true that compound chocolate has little flavour, it does not require tempering. If you stick to a well-known brand, you can safely use it for decorative purposes, getting flavour from 'pure' chocolate used elsewhere in the dish.

Chewy Fudge Cookies

625 g (20 oz) dark (plain or semisweet) chocolate, cut into small chunks
125 g (4 oz) milk cooking chocolate, chopped
125 g (4 oz) unsalted butter
3 large eggs
$3\frac{1}{2}$ tablespoons soft (light) brown sugar
1 cup (250 g, 8 oz) granulated sugar
a level $\frac{3}{4}$ cup (80 g, $2\frac{3}{4}$ oz) plain (all-purpose) flour
$\frac{1}{4}$ teaspoon baking powder
1 cup (125 g, 4 oz) chopped walnuts *or* pecans

Preheat the oven to 180°C (350°F). Line several baking sheets with baking parchment.

Place 1 cup (200 g, 7 oz) of the dark chocolate, all of the milk chocolate and the butter in a large microwave mixing bowl. Heat in the microwave at 100% (high) for 2 minutes.*

Place the eggs, brown sugar and granulated sugar in a mixing bowl. Whisk until pale and fluffy, and a thin ribbon forms when the beaters are lifted from the mixture. Sift the flour and baking powder together.

Remove the chocolate mixture from the microwave and stir to combine all the ingredients. Fold into the whisked egg mixture with the sifted flour until well combined, then gently fold in the remaining chocolate chunks and the nuts. Cover and chill the mixture for 20 minutes.

Drop generous amounts of the mixture per cookie onto the tray (about $\frac{1}{4}$ cup or 3 tablespoons each), leaving 6–7 cm ($2\frac{1}{4}$–$2\frac{1}{2}$ in) between each cookie. Do not flatten the mixture.

Bake in the oven for 15–18 minutes. The cookies will feel barely baked and a thin, cracked layer should show on the top. At this stage, the cookies will remain nice, soft eating cookies. Bake longer for crisp cookies if desired.

Allow to cool on the tray. Do not keep for more than 3 days.

Makes 12

*If you don't have a microwave, melt the chocolate and butter in a metal bowl sitting over a saucepan of simmering water. Stir until melted and combined.

Chocolate Macaroon Sticks

2 large egg whites
1/2 cup (125 g, 4 oz) caster (superfine) sugar
2 tablespoons drinking chocolate
1 2/3 cups (150 g, 5 oz) desiccated (shredded) coconut
2 tablespoons cocoa, sifted
1/2 cup (90 g, 3 oz) icing (confectioners') sugar, plus extra for dusting
2 tablespoons hot water

Preheat the oven to 160°C (325°F). Lightly grease two baking sheets.

Whisk the egg whites until stiff peaks form.

Mix the caster sugar with the drinking chocolate and, whisking continuously, very slowly add to the egg whites. Whisk until stiff. Stir in the coconut.

Using a piping (pastry) bag fitted with a 1 cm (3/8 in) plain round nozzle, pipe the mixture into 5 cm (2 in) lengths onto the prepared sheets.

Bake in the oven for 35–40 minutes. Allow to cool on the baking sheets.

Mix the cocoa, icing sugar and hot water in a saucepan and warm for a few seconds over a low heat.

Dip one end of the baked macaroon sticks into the icing, then place onto a sheet of baking parchment to dry. Dust the other end of each stick with icing sugar before serving.

Makes 15–18

Chocolate Pioneers
Laura Ingersoll Secord

A British–Canadian heroine in the 1812–13 war against the United States. In June 1813, Laura Secord, seeing US troops passing her home on the Niagara Peninsula, walked 20 miles through enemy lines to warn nearby British forces. A century later, the Laura Secord Chocolate company was formed in Toronto, its name commemorating Secord's deed.

Chocolate
Sugar Delights

185 g (6 oz) unsalted butter, softened

1 cup (185 g, 6 oz) soft (light) brown sugar

3 tablespoons golden syrup

1 large egg

2 cups (250 g, 8 oz) plain (all-purpose) flour

2 teaspoons baking powder

2 tablespoons cocoa powder

2 teaspoons ground cinnamon

raw or demerara sugar

Cream the butter, sugar and golden syrup together until light and fluffy. Add the egg and combine thoroughly.

Sift the flour, baking powder, cocoa powder and cinnamon together and add to the butter mixture in two batches. Combine thoroughly. Cover the dough with cling film (plastic wrap) and refrigerate for 45 minutes.

Preheat the oven to 180°C (350°F). Line a baking sheet with baking parchment.

Take walnut-size portions of the dough and roll into balls. Roll half of each ball in raw sugar and place on the prepared sheet. Keep the cookies apart as they will spread considerably during cooking.

Bake in the oven for 10–12 minutes. Remove from the oven and allow to cool slightly on the tray before sliding onto a wire rack to cool completely.

Makes about 24

What is the best chocolate for cooking?

Most recipes specify a preferred style or variety, but you should not be afraid to substitute a couverture or pure chocolate of your choice – the truth is that it is not the chocolate that creates the better cake, but the chef.

Chocolate Tuiles

7 large egg whites
1 cup (185 g, 6 oz) icing (confectioners') sugar
1/2 cup (60 g, 2 oz) plain (all-purpose) flour
1/4 cup (30 g, 1 oz) cocoa powder
75 g (2 1/2 oz) unsalted butter, melted
flaked (sliced) almonds, for decoration

Preheat the oven to 180°C (350°F). Lightly grease baking sheets.

Whisk the egg whites with the icing sugar until well incorporated. Add the flour and cocoa powder, and whisk again. Let the batter rest for 10–15 minutes and then stir in the butter.

Place small amounts of the batter on the prepared sheets and spread thinly. Bake in the oven for 5–8 minutes. (It is better to judge when they are cooked by touch rather than by colour.)

Once baked, remove carefully but quickly from the sheet using a flat palette knife and roll each tuile over a rolling pin or other utensil to give a curved shape. While the tuiles are setting, press flaked almonds into them to decorate. Slide off the rolling pin when cool and hard.

Makes 12

How to Taste Chocolate

Price, personal taste and brand reputation are common considerations for anyone purchasing chocolate. Like wine, however, chocolate has a number of other characteristics that the true connoisseur considers when assessing its quality. The following guide will enable the ordinary consumer to evaluate chocolate using the same criteria as the judges of international competitions. Of course, if you lack the time or the restraint to analyse your chocolate, you can safely bet that if it looks good, smells good and tastes good, it is probably an acceptable chocolate.

Appearance

A high gloss and a smooth unblemished surface are both signs of a good chocolate. If the chocolate is lacklustre or dull, or become grey, spotty or distorted, it has probably suffered from 'heat stress' during its manufacture or transportation.

Feel

Fine chocolate, when touched, melts easily and rapidly. The faster a chocolate melts, the higher its concentration of cocoa butter or natural fat — expensive ingredients which are practically absent in the lower grade product.

Sound

A good-quality, well-conditioned and properly tempered chocolate should produce a solid 'crack' when broken. A limp, bendable fracture indicates that the chocolate is either in a poor condition or manufactured with low-quality, substitute fats.

Aroma

To judge aroma, leave a small chunk of chocolate in an airtight jar for 24 to 48 hours. Carefully unscrew the lid and press your nose over the jar. The aroma should be delicate, sweet (though not cloying) and redolent of cocoa.

Taste

The connoisseur never 'eats' chocolate, but places it on the tongue before pausing for it to melt and 'introducing' it to the body. A little air inhaled through the corner of the lips enhances what should be a full-bodied flavour throughout the mouth. The flavours of chocolates are 'notes', and, like wine, often require time to develop fullness and 'finish'.

Spicy Fingers

400 g (14 oz) unsalted butter

1½ cups (375 mL, 12 fl oz) golden syrup *or* dark corn syrup

1 large egg

1 cup (185 g, 6 oz) soft (light) brown sugar

3½ cups (435 g, 14 oz) plain (all-purpose) flour

1½ teaspoons bicarbonate of soda (baking soda)

1½ teaspoons ground ginger

1½ teaspoons ground cinnamon

½ cup (125 mL, 4 fl oz) boiling water

2 tablespoons sour cream

225 g (7 oz) chocolate chips (drops) *or* dark (plain or semisweet) chocolate, finely chopped

icing (confectioners') sugar, for dusting

Preheat the oven to 180°C (350°F). Grease a 35 x 30 x 3 cm (14 x 12 x 1¼ in) baking sheet with baking parchment.

Heat the butter and golden syrup in a saucepan over a gentle heat until melted. Add the egg and brown sugar, stirring continuously.

Sift the flour, bicarbonate of soda, ginger and cinnamon together into a bowl.

Add the egg mixture and boiling water, and mix quickly until smooth. Now add the sour cream and chocolate chips, and stir through.

Spread the mixture onto the prepared sheet and bake in the oven for 25–35 minutes, or until a skewer inserted into the centre comes out clean.

Allow to cool on the tray, then dust with icing sugar before cutting into fingers.

Makes 24

Great Moments in Chocolate

1832 A 16-year-old cook, Franz Sacher, produces the first Sacher Torte, for Duke Metternich of Austria. The dish remains unknown to the general public until 1888.

Triple Chocolate Spice Cookies

185 g (6 oz) unsalted butter, softened

1 cup (185 g, 6 oz) soft (light) brown sugar

$\frac{1}{3}$ cup (90 mL, 3 fl oz) golden syrup *or* dark corn syrup

1 large egg

2 cups (250 g, 8 oz) plain (all-purpose) flour

2 teaspoons baking powder

2 tablespoons cocoa powder

2 teaspoons ground cinnamon

30 g (1 oz) white chocolate, finely chopped, plus extra
melted chocolate for drizzling

30 g (1 oz) milk chocolate, finely chopped, plus extra
melted chocolate for drizzling

dark (plain or semisweet) chocolate, melted, for drizzling

Cream the butter, brown sugar and golden syrup until light and fluffy. Add the egg and mix until combined.

Sift the flour, baking powder, cocoa powder and cinnamon together into a bowl. Add to the creamed mixture in two batches. Mix well.

Fold in the finely chopped white and milk chocolates. Cover the dough with cling film (plastic wrap) and refrigerate for 45 minutes.

Preheat the oven to 180°C (350°F). Line a baking sheet with baking parchment.

Remove the dough from the refrigerator. Take walnut-size portions of the dough, roll into balls and place on the prepared sheets. Allow at least 5 cm (2 in) between each cookie for spreading. Bake in the oven for 12–15 minutes.

Remove from the oven and allow to cool slightly on the sheet before placing on a wire cooling rack.

Once the cookies are cool, drizzle each one with a small amount of the melted white, milk and dark chocolates.

Makes 24

Chocolate, like life, should be
approached with a passionate,
yet reckless abandon.

Anonymous

singularly
indulgent

pastries &
chocolates

Chocolate Bread

7 cups (875 g, 1¾ lb) plain (all-purpose) flour, sifted
1 cup (100 g, 3½ oz) cocoa powder, sifted
½ cup (125 g, 4 oz) sugar
30 g (1 oz) fresh compressed yeast
8 large eggs
1 cup (250 mL, 8 fl oz) milk, warm
375 g (12 oz) unsalted butter

Place the flour and cocoa into a mixing bowl with the sugar. Add the yeast to the warm milk and stir until dissolved. Whisk the eggs into the yeast mixture and combine with the flour mixture.

Mix to a dough and knead for several minutes (5–6 minutes). When the dough is smooth, add the butter and continue working until all the butter is incorporated.

Remove the dough to a larger bowl and cover tightly with cling film (plastic wrap). Refrigerate for 8 hours or overnight.

Grease two 23 x 13 cm (9 x 5 in) loaf pans. Remove the dough from the refrigerator and divide in half. Knead each piece lightly and then place into prepared pans.

Prove the dough for 45–50 minutes, or until doubled in bulk. Preheat the oven to 200°C (400°F).

Bake the loaves in the oven for 45–50 minutes. Allow to cool in the pans for 5 minutes before turning out and standing on a wire rack until cold.

Makes 2 loaves

Chocolate Pioneers
François Louis Cailler
The founding father of the Swiss chocolate industry.
Having seen chocolate for the first time at a country fair,
Cailler spent four years working in the Caffarel chocolate
factory in Milan. In 1819, at the age of 23, he opened the
first Swiss chocolate factory at Corsier, near Vevey,
using stone rollers of his own design.

Chocolate Choc Chip Muffins

3 cups (375 g, 12 oz) plain (all-purpose) flour
3 tablespoons cocoa powder
1 tablespoon baking powder
1½ cups (250 g, 8 oz) soft (light) brown sugar
225 g (7 oz) dark (plain or semisweet) chocolate, chopped
1½ cups (375 mL, 12 fl oz) milk
125 g (4 oz) butter, melted
2 large eggs, lightly beaten

Preheat the oven to 180°C (350°F). Grease a 5 cm (2 in) muffin cup pan.

Sift the flour, cocoa powder and baking powder into a large bowl.

Add the brown sugar and dark chocolate. Stir to combine.

Stir in the milk, butter and eggs. Mix thoroughly.

Spoon the batter into the muffin cup pan and bake in the oven for 20–25 minutes.

Allow to cool slightly before turning out of the pan. Serve hot with butter.

Makes about 15

Choc-Cross Buns

1 cup (250 mL, 8 fl oz) water
2 tablespoons dried milk (or skim milk) powder
3 cups (375 g, 12 oz) plain (all-purpose) flour
5 teaspoons caster (superfine) sugar
$\frac{1}{2}$ teaspoon ground cinnamon
$\frac{1}{2}$ teaspoon ground cloves
60 g (2 oz) unsalted butter
30 g (1 oz) fresh compressed yeast
1 large egg
100 g ($3\frac{1}{2}$ oz) chocolate chips
2 tablespoons sultanas (golden raisins)
2 tablespoons mixed (candied) peel

Cross Mixture

1 cup (125 g, 4 oz) plain (all-purpose) flour
1 tablespoon cocoa powder
5–6 tablespoons water

Glaze

2 tablespoons water
2 tablespoons powder gelatin
2 tablespoons caster (superfine) sugar

Lightly grease a 30 x 25 x 3 cm (12 x 10 x $1\frac{3}{4}$ in) baking pan.

Mix the water with the dried milk powder and lightly whisk until well combined.

Place the flour, caster sugar and spices in a separate bowl. Rub in the butter and yeast with your fingers until the mixture resemble fresh breadcrumbs. Stir in the milk mixture and egg, and work into a dough.

Remove the dough from the bowl and knead it quickly and lightly on a lightly floured surface for 5 minutes. Lightly knead through the chocolate chips, sultanas and mixed peel.

Return the dough to the bowl and cover with a damp cloth. Place the bowl in a warm place for 40 minutes, or until the dough has doubled in size.

Remove the dough from the bowl and knock back (punch down) into a solid mass again. Make sure you get rid of all the air bubbles. Cut the dough into 16 small pieces and roll them into balls. Place the balls onto the prepared tray and put in a warm area for 30–40 minutes, or until they have again doubled in size.

Preheat the oven to 200°C (400°F).

While the buns are rising, make the cross mixture. Mix the flour, cocoa powder and enough of the water together so that the mixture is stiff enough to hold its shape when piped.

When the buns have doubled in size, pipe the cross mixture over the buns in a cross shape using a piping bag. Bake in the oven for 30–45 minutes, or until golden brown.

Just before the buns are cooked, make the glaze. Bring the water, powdered gelatin and caster sugar to the boil in a saucepan. You need to use this glaze as soon as it is made.

When the buns are cooked, brush their tops immediately with the glaze. Allow to cool.

Makes 16

Chocolate Pioneers
Jean Tobler

After opening his shop in Bern, Switzerland, in 1868, Jean Tobler sold so many chocolates that circumstances almost forced him to become a chocolate manufacturer. In 1899 he founded the 'Fabrique de Chocolate, Tobler & Cie'. The company's most famed product was the Toblerone bar, which is still widely popular today.

Using Leftover Melted Chocolate

The only pitfall in making chocolates and truffles is that there is always leftover chocolate from breakages, drips and mistakes, usually with other ingredients in it. This scrap chocolate cannot be returned to your pot of good, smooth chocolate. Instead of wasting leftover chocolate, why not use it to make some of the following delicious treats?

Chocolate Florentines

This is a simple recipe for using up any leftover chocolate. Remelt the chocolate and spoon it in small, rounded mounds onto a baking sheet lined with baking parchment. Press small pieces of glacé (candied) pineapple, glacé cherry and whole brazil nuts into the top of the chocolate mounds. Allow the mounds to set firm in the refrigerator, then peel off the baking parchment and dust the florentines lightly with icing (confectioners') sugar.

Chocolate Fingers

One of the simplest ways to use leftover chocolate is to add one or two drops of an oil-based flavouring such as peppermint. Stir through the chocolate, then pour the mixture onto a baking sheet lined with baking parchment and allow to set. Once firm, cut the chocolate into fingers about 5 cm x 1 cm (2 in x $\frac{3}{8}$ in). Serve with coffee for a wicked treat.

Chocolate Fruit Bark

One of the several ways in which to use leftover chocolate is to remelt it and add extra fruit and nuts. The type and amount is up to you. After adding these ingredients, spread the mixture onto a sheet of baking parchment on a baking sheet. Press more fruit and nuts onto the top and allow the chocolate to set hard in the refrigerator. Once set, simply break into small bite-size pieces and serve.

Chocolate Tuiles

Another way to use leftover melted chocolate is spoon it onto small squares of plastic — about 5 cm x 5 cm (2 in x 2 in) — cut from plastic bags. Use a spatula to spread the chocolate into round discs before draping the plastic over a rolling pin or cylindrical object and allowing the chocolate to set. Once firm, carefully peel away the plastic from the chocolate. Dust the chocolate tuiles with icing (confectioners') sugar and serve.

Chocolate Leaves

Spread a thin amount of melted chocolate onto clean fresh leaves. Allow the chocolate to set before peeling away the leaves. For best results, the leaves need to be shiny and well veined in texture. Should the leaves stick to the chocolate, oil them and repeat the process.

Chocolate Nut Clusters

Roast some finely chopped nuts of your choice on a baking sheet until they are a light golden brown. Allow to cool, then spoon small amounts of leftover melted chocolate onto the cooled nuts and stir in, flattening the mixture as you do so. Place small spoonfuls of the chocolate-covered nuts on another baking sheet lined with baking parchment, then chill in the refrigerator until the clusters are set firm. If you wish, you can also add dried fruit or candied peel; fold this through the chocolate nut clusters before spooning onto the sheet to set.

Quick Coconut Clusters

Add enough toasted shredded (flaked) coconut to a bowl of leftover melted chocolate to stiffen the mixture until it is of a consistency that will hold its shape and can be spooned onto baking parchment. Allow the clusters to set firm in the refrigerator. Once they are hard, dip them into clean melted dark (plain or semisweet) chocolate. Drizzle with melted chocolate of a different colour, or roll them in cocoa powder, icing (confectioners') sugar or drinking chocolate before serving with strong coffee.

Chocolate Cream Puffs

1 cup (250 mL, 8 fl oz) water
90 g (3 oz) unsalted butter
1 level cup (100 g, 3½ oz) plain (all-purpose) flour, sifted
2 tablespoons cocoa powder, sifted
4–5 large eggs
1 quantity Creamy Chocolate Mousse (see page 134)
icing (confectioners') sugar or cocoa powder, for dusting

Preheat the oven to 200°C (400°F). Lightly grease a baking sheet.

Bring the water and butter slowly to the boil in a saucepan. While the mixture is boiling, stir in the flour and cocoa. Continue stirring vigorously as the mixture cooks, until it leaves the sides of the pan and forms a solid ball (about 2 minutes). Remove from the heat.

Beat in 4 eggs one at a time, until the mixture becomes smooth and shiny. Stop beating and run a pipe or knife through the mixture. If it leaves a definite trail that only just starts to cover over itself, the consistency is perfect. It should not be any thinner than this. (If required, add the last egg.)

Place large tablespoons of the batter onto the prepared tray and bake in the oven for 35–40 minutes. To prevent steam from escaping, do not open the oven door for the first 15 minutes.

When cooked, pierce a small hole in the base of each puff to allow internal steam to escape. Allow the puffs to cool. Scoop out any uncooked mixture.

When cold, cut in half and fill with the Creamy Chocolate Mousse. Dust the top of the puffs with icing sugar or cocoa, or a mixture of both.

Makes 12

What is meant by the terms 'semisweet' and 'bitter' chocolate?

US and Continental recipes often use these terms, which refer to different varieties of what is known elsewhere simply as dark chocolate. The sugar content of dark chocolate equates with the semisweet variety, so if you encounter a recipe that requires bitter-sweet or bitter, use dark chocolate and slightly reduce the recipe's sugar content.

Chocolate Peanut Doughnuts

This recipe was given to me at a demonstration by a woman who wanted to see them made, but did not want to go to the bother of cooking them for herself. After making three batches in the same day and having them all disappear within seconds, we decided that this recipe was an outstanding success.

3$\frac{1}{2}$ cups (453 g, 14 oz) plain (all-purpose) flour

$\frac{3}{4}$ cup (125 g, 4 oz) unsalted dry-roast peanuts

1 cup (250 g, 8 oz) sugar

2 teaspoons baking powder

1$\frac{1}{2}$ teaspoons salt

$\frac{3}{4}$ cup (185 mL, 8 fl oz) milk

1 large egg

3 tablespoons vegetable oil

2 teaspoons vanilla essence (extract)

extra vegetable oil, for frying

Chocolate Glaze

500 g (1 lb) dark (plain or semisweet) chocolate

$\frac{3}{4}$ cup (185 mL, 6 fl oz) water

$\frac{1}{4}$ cup (60 g, 2 oz) sugar

2 tablespoons liquid glucose

chopped unsalted peanuts

In a food processor fitted with a metal chopping blade, combine $\frac{1}{2}$ cup (60g, 2 oz) of the flour with the peanuts. Process until coarsely chopped. In a large bowl, mix together the remaining flour, the peanut mixture, sugar, baking powder and salt.

Whisk together the milk, egg, oil and vanilla essence, and pour into the centre of the dry ingredients. Combine all the ingredients and work into a dough. Knead on a lightly floured surface — do not overwork, 6–7 times is plenty.

Flatten the dough onto a sheet of baking parchment and press out to 1$\frac{1}{2}$ cm ($\frac{3}{4}$ in) in thickness. Cover the dough with cling film (plastic wrap) and freeze for 30 minutes, or until firm.

Using a floured 7 cm (2$\frac{1}{2}$ in) plain cookie cutter, cut out discs from the flattened dough and cut a smaller hole from the centre of each of these (approximately 2 cm ($\frac{3}{4}$ in) in diameter). Place the doughnuts and holes onto a baking sheet lined with baking parchment. Refrigerate for 2–3 hours. Remove from the refrigerator and let stand for 15 minutes at room temperature before frying.

Heat the extra vegetable oil to 180°C (350°F). Fry one doughnut at a time until golden brown, then turn over and cook on the other side for about 1 minute. Drain on absorbent kitchen paper (paper towels) and allow to cool.

To make the chocolate glaze, melt the chocolate over a pot of simmering water. Mix the water, sugar and liquid glucose in a saucepan and stir over a gentle heat until the sugar is completely dissolved — do not allow it to boil. Remove from the heat. Mix the sugar syrup with the chocolate and stir well.

Set the glaze over a pot of simmering water to keep warm. Drop the cooled doughnuts onto the surface of the glaze. Using a fork, flip them over to cover both sides with the glaze. Remove to a wire rack and sprinkle the chopped peanuts on top.

Refrigerate for 15 minutes to harden the glaze and then serve immediately. These doughnuts will keep for 1–2 days if stored in an airtight container.

Makes 14 doughnuts and 14 holes

Chocolate Pioneers
The Callebaut Family

The Callebaut Company was established in 1850 when the Callebaut family opened a malt plant, brewery and dairy. In 1890, they moved into confectionery production and in 1911, chocolate production. By the 1960s, the Callebaut family had established a worldwide reputation for the quality of their couverture chocolate, and sales have continued to expand.

Orange Chocolate Madeleines

150 g (5 oz) unsalted butter, softened
1 1/4 cups (225 g, 7 oz) icing (confectioners') sugar, sifted
3 large eggs
1 1/2 cups (185 g, 6 oz) plain (all-purpose) flour
3 tablespoons cocoa powder
1 teaspoon baking powder
1 tablespoon freshly squeezed orange juice
finely grated zest of 1 orange
extra icing (confectioners') sugar, for dusting

Preheat the oven to 180°C (350°F). Lightly grease a madeleine pan.

Cream the butter and icing sugar until light and fluffy. Add the eggs one at a time, beating well after each addition.

Sift in the flour, cocoa and baking powder, then add the orange juice and zest. Mix thoroughly.

Fill the madeleine moulds with the batter until each mould is three-quarters full. Bake in the oven for 20–25 minutes, or until each madeleine is springy to the touch.

When baked, unmould immediately and dust lightly with the extra icing sugar before serving warm.

Makes about 24

If any man has drunk a little too deeply
from the cup of physical pleasure;
if he has spent too much time at his desk
that should have been spent asleep;
if his fine spirits have temporarily
become dulled;
if he finds the air too damp, the minutes
too slow, and the atmosphere
too heavy to withstand;
if he is obsessed by a fixed idea which
bars him from any freedom of thought:
if he is any of these poor
creatures, we say,
let him be given a good pint of amber-
flavoured chocolate, in the proportions
of sixty to seventy-two grains
of amber to a pound, and marvels
will be performed.

Brillat-Savarin, *Physiologie du Gout*, 1825

Orange Streusel Muffins

3 cups (375 g, 12 oz) plain (all-purpose) flour

3 tablespoons cocoa powder

1 tablespoon baking powder

1½ cups (250 g, 8 oz) soft (light) brown sugar

100 g (3 1/2 oz) chocolate chips (drops) *or* dark (plain or semisweet chocolate), finely chopped

finely grated zest and juice of 1 large orange

1¼ cups (310 mL, 10 fl oz) milk

125 g (4 oz) unsalted butter, melted

2 large eggs

Streusel Topping

½ cup (60 g, 2 oz) plain (all-purpose) flour

1 teaspoon ground cinnamon

¼ cup (30 g, 1 oz) ground almonds

5 teaspoons caster (superfine) sugar

60 g (2 oz) unsalted butter

icing (confectioners') sugar, for dusting

Preheat the oven to 160°C (325°F). Grease a patty or small muffin pan well with butter.

Sift the flour, cocoa powder and baking powder into a bowl. Stir in the brown sugar and chocolate chips.

Mix the orange juice and zest, milk, butter and eggs into the dry ingredients until thoroughly combined.

Pour the batter into the cake or muffin moulds until each mould is three-quarters full.

To make the streusel topping, place the flour, cinnamon, ground almonds and sugar in a mixing bowl. Rub in the butter until the mixture resembles fresh breadcrumbs.

Sprinkle a little of the streusel on top of each mould of muffin batter. Bake in the oven 20–25 minutes.

Allow the muffins to cool in the pan for 10 minutes before carefully turning out. Cool on a wire rack and dust lightly with icing sugar.

Makes 15

Chocolate Cups

The paper cases used to produce these chocolate cups are available in most department store cookery sections, in specialist chocolate or confectionery stores and in homeware or kitchen stores.

50–60 petit four paper cases or cups

310 g (10 oz) dark (plain or semisweet) chocolate, melted

Filling

225 g (7 oz) milk chocolate

2 cups (500 mL, 1 imp. pint) double (heavy, thickened) cream

dark (plain or semisweet) chocolate, for decorating

Separate the petit four cases into stacks of two or three to strengthen them and place on a baking sheet.

Dip your finger into the melted dark chocolate and coat the inside of each case. When this layer of chocolate has set, repeat the process. Make certain that the chocolate is spread to the rim of the case, but does not spill over or sit on top of the rim — this makes removal difficult. Allow the cases to set firm in the refrigerator while making the filling.

Very carefully peel away the cases from each chocolate cup. If the chocolate is softened by the heat of your hands, return the cups to the refrigerator for several minutes.

To make the filling, melt the milk chocolate until smooth and warm. Add the cream and whisk very quickly so that the chocolate does not set firm. Continue whisking until a smooth paste has formed. (If the mixture looks split or curdled, or sets hard, place over a pot of simmering water and stir until completely melted and smooth.)

Allow the filling to cool completely before spooning into the chocolate cups, adding extra cream to the mixture if it is not of pouring consistency. Fill each cup to the brim and return to the baking sheet. When all the cups have been filled, place the baking sheet in the refrigerator for 1 hour.

Using a paper piping bag, cut so that the tip is just fine enough for the chocolate to drizzle from, drizzle a small amount of the melted dark chocolate over the top of each filled cup. Serve with coffee, or float one in your coffee and allow it to melt as you drink.

Makes 50–60

The only way to get rid

of a temptation

is to yield to it.

Oscar Wilde
The Picture of Dorian Gray

lusciously
lustful

tortes
& cakes

Mother's Flourless Chocolate Cake

125 g (4 oz) unsalted butter
½ cup (125 g, 4 oz) sugar
5 large eggs, separated
225 g (7 oz) dark (plain or semisweet) chocolate, grated
1⅓ cups (150 g, 5 oz) ground almonds
finely grated zest of 1 lemon

Preheat the oven to 180°C (350°F). Lightly grease a 20 cm (8 in) springform cake pan and line the bottom with baking parchment.

Cream the butter and sugar until light and fluffy. Add the egg yolks one at a time, beating well between each addition.

Add the dark chocolate, then fold through the almonds and lemon zest.

In a separate bowl, whisk the egg whites until frothy and stiff peaks begin to form. Fold the egg whites through the cake batter. Pour into the prepared cake pan and bake in the oven for 35 minutes, or until the top of the cake is firm to touch. Do not remove from the pan.

Allow the cake to cool, then refrigerate for 2 hours before removing from the pan. Serve with a marinated berry mixture and double (heavy) cream.

Store in an airtight container. This cake is best served and eaten the day it is made, but will keep for 2–3 days.

Serves 8–10

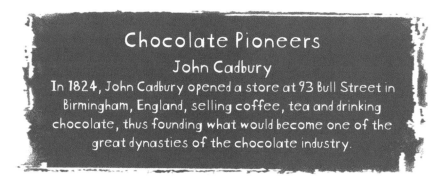

Chocolate Pioneers
John Cadbury
In 1824, John Cadbury opened a store at 93 Bull Street in Birmingham, England, selling coffee, tea and drinking chocolate, thus founding what would become one of the great dynasties of the chocolate industry.

Chocolate Beetroot Cake

4 large eggs, separated

¾ cup (125 g, 4 oz) icing (confectioners') sugar

100 g (3½ oz) grated beetroot (beet)

1⅔ cups (185 g, 6 oz) ground almonds

2 tablespoons plain (all-purpose) flour

1 tablespoon cocoa powder

1½ teaspoons baking powder

finely grated zest of 1 lemon

½ cup (125 mL, 4 fl oz) sugar syrup (see below)

finely grated zest and juice of 1 orange

250 g (8 oz) Chocolate Buttercream (see page 106)

125 g (4 oz) dark (plain or semisweet) chocolate, shaved

Preheat the oven to 180°C (350°F). Lightly grease a 23 cm (9 in) springform cake pan and line the bottom with baking parchment.

Place the egg yolks and half of the icing sugar in a mixing bowl and whisk lightly. Place the egg whites and the remaining icing sugar in a separate bowl and whisk until stiff peaks form.

Fold the beetroot, ground almonds, flour, cocoa, baking powder and lemon zest into the yolk mixture, then fold through the egg whites.

Pour the batter into the prepared cake pan and bake in the oven for 40–45 minutes. Turn the cake out of the pan and allow to cool on a wire rack.

Mix the sugar syrup and orange juice and zest together in a bowl. Cut the cake in half horizontally and brush both cut sides with the syrup.

Sandwich the cake together with the Chocolate Buttercream. Cover the top and sides with the remaining buttercream and decorate with the chocolate shavings. Refrigerate for 1 hour before serving.

Serves 12

Sugar Syrup

Bring ⅔ cup (150 mL, 5 fl oz) water and ⅔ cup (150 g, 5 oz) sugar to the boil in a saucepan, stirring occasionally until the sugar dissolves. Allow to cool and set aside until ready to use.

Chocolate Ginger Sponge

125 g (4 oz) unsalted butter
½ cup (125 g, 4 oz) caster (superfine) sugar
1 tablespoon fresh ginger, finely grated
5 large eggs, separated
60 g (2 oz) dark (plain or semisweet) chocolate, melted
3 tablespoons cocoa powder, sifted
1¼ cups (150 g, 5 oz) plain (all-purpose) flour, sifted
1 teaspoon baking powder
1½ tablespoons dark rum
icing (confectioners') sugar, for dusting

Preheat the oven to 180°C (350°F). Lightly grease a 20 cm (8 in) springform cake pan and line the bottom with baking parchment.

Cream the butter and ¼ cup (60 g, 2 oz) of the caster sugar with the ginger until light and fluffy. Add the egg yolks one at a time, beating well between additions.

Add the dark chocolate to the creamed mixture, mixing quickly to ensure the chocolate is combined before it hardens, then add the cocoa, flour and baking powder, and combine well.

In a separate bowl, whisk the egg whites until frothy and stiff peaks begin to form. Slowly add the remaining ¼ cup (60 g, 2 oz) caster sugar, whisking continuously as you do so. Keep whisking until all the sugar has dissolved. Carefully and thoroughly fold the rum and the egg white mixture through the cake batter.

Pour the mixture into the prepared cake pan and bake in the oven for 35–40 minutes, or until a skewer inserted into the top of the cake comes out clean.

Allow the cake to cool in the pan slightly. Remove and dust lightly with the icing sugar before serving warm and fresh.

If stored in an airtight container, this cake will keep for 2–3 days.

Serves 8–10

Chocolate Kugelhopf

225 g (7 oz) dark (plain or semisweet) chocolate

1 cup (250 mL, 8 fl oz) golden syrup or corn syrup

250 g (8 oz) butter, softened

1/4 cup (60 g, 2 oz) caster (superfine) sugar

4 large eggs

2 1/2 cups (310 g, 10 oz) plain (all-purpose) flour, sifted

1 teaspoon baking powder

cocoa powder and icing (confectioners') sugar, for dusting

chocolate leaves, for decorating (see page 64)

Preheat the oven to 160°C (325°F). Grease a kugelhopf ring mould well with butter.

Melt the cooking chocolate in a heatproof bowl over hot water (or in the microwave on medium 50% for 3–4 minutes). Stir in the golden syrup. Remove from the heat and set aside.

Cream the butter and sugar until light and fluffy. Add the eggs one at a time, beating well between each addition.

Sift the flour and the baking powder together, then alternately add the flour and the cooled chocolate mixture to the creamed mixture. Combine well.

Pour the batter into the kugelhopf mould and bake in the oven for 1–1 1/4 hours, or until a metal skewer inserted into the top of the cake comes out clean.

Turn the cake out of the pan and allow to cool on a wire rack. Dust with cocoa and icing sugar, and decorate with the chocolate leaves.

This cake will keep for up to a week if stored in an airtight container.

Serves 10–12

Chocolate Hungarian Torte

5 large eggs, separated

¾ cup (185 g, 6 oz) caster (superfine) sugar

410 g (14 oz) dark (plain or semisweet) chocolate, melted

⅓ cup (90 mL, 3 fl oz) milk

1¼ cups (150 g, 5 oz) plain (all-purpose) flour, sifted

2 cups (225 g, 7 oz) ground almonds

2 tablespoons apricot jam

225 g (7 oz) marzipan or almond paste

500 g (1 lb) dark (plain or semisweet) chocolate buttons, melted

500 g (1 lb) white chocolate buttons, melted

Preheat the oven to 150°C (300°F). Lightly grease a 20 cm (8 in) springform cake pan and line the bottom with baking parchment.

Beat the egg yolks with ½ cup (125 g, 4 oz) of the caster sugar until thick and pale. Gently fold in the dark chocolate by hand, then add the milk, flour and ground almonds.

In a separate bowl, beat the egg whites until frothy and very stiff peaks form. Slowly add the remaining ¼ cup (60 g, 2 oz) caster sugar, whisking continuously as you do so. Keep whisking until all the sugar has dissolved. Gently fold into the chocolate mixture.

Pour the mixture into the prepared cake pan and bake in the oven for 30–40 minutes, or until the top of the cake springs back when lightly touched. Allow to cool in the pan on a wire rack.

When completely cold, turn the cake out of the pan and remove the baking parchment from the bottom. Thinly spread the top and sides of the cake with the apricot jam.

On a lightly floured surface, roll the marzipan into a circle large enough to cover the top and sides of the cake. Place the marzipan over the cake and mould to fit neatly. Trim away any excess marzipan.

To make the chocolate collar, cut a strip of baking parchment long enough to wrap around the cake and protrude 1 cm (½ in) above its top. Spread half of the melted dark chocolate buttons onto the baking parchment. Wrap the chocolate collar around the cake. Allow the cake to stand in the refrigerator for 5 minutes or until the collar is firm. Use the remaining dark chocolate buttons and half the white chocolate buttons to make chocolate curls. Set aside and allow to set.

Remove the baking parchment from the chocolate collar once it is set. Drizzle the remaining white chocolate on the collar and decorate the cake with the chocolate curls.

This torte will keep for up to a week in an airtight container in the refrigerator.

Serves 12

Chocolate Pavlova

4 large egg whites

¼ cup (50 g, 1¾ oz) icing (confectioners') sugar, sifted

1¼ cups (225 g, 7 oz) caster (superfine) sugar

1 teaspoon white vinegar

3 tablespoons cornflour (cornstarch)

3 tablespoons cocoa powder

pinch of salt

1¼ cups (310 mL, 10 fl oz) cream, freshly whipped

fresh fruits of your choice

Preheat the oven to 90°C (175°F). Line a baking sheet with foil and lightly dust with cornflour.

Using an electric mixer, whisk the egg whites until they are frothy and stiff peaks form. Combine the icing sugar and the caster sugar, and slowly add to the egg whites, whisking continuously until the sugar has completely dissolved. Fold in the vinegar and cornflour, then fold in the cocoa powder and salt.

Spread the mixture into a 20 cm (8 in) circle on the prepared baking sheet, place in the oven and bake for 2 hours.

Turn the oven off and allow the pavlova to remain in the oven. When both the oven and the pavlova are cold, remove the pavlova.

Top with the freshly whipped cream and fresh fruits of your choice.

This pavlova can be made ahead of time (up to 2–3 days) and stored in an airtight container (not in the refrigerator) prior to decoration.

Once covered with cream, the pavlova should be consumed within 24 hours.

Serves 8–10

Should I add oil or fat to thin chocolate for use as a topping or glaze?

Some recipes suggest you add oils or fats such as butter to chocolate in this way. Remember that fats and oils break down the natural structure of chocolate, ruining it for piping or flood work. Thinning may still be worthwhile, but bear in mind that a good stir can be equally effective.

Chocolate
Pear Shortcake

300 g (10 oz) unsalted butter
1½ cups (300 g, 10 oz) caster (superfine) sugar
3 large eggs
1½ cups (185 g, 6 oz) plain (all-purpose) flour
2 tablespoons cocoa powder
1 teaspoon ground cinnamon
1 teaspoon mixed spice (see note below)
1 teaspoon baking powder
310 g (10 oz) canned pears, sliced
icing (confectioners') sugar, for dusting

Preheat the oven to 180°C (350°F). Lightly grease a 23 cm (9 in) springform cake pan and line the bottom with baking parchment.

Cream the butter and sugar until light and fluffy. Add the eggs one at a time, beating well between each addition. Sift the flour, cocoa, cinnamon, mixed spice and baking powder into the mixture. Continue mixing until well incorporated.

Spread half of the mixture evenly over the bottom of the cake pan — it may be a firm paste, so it will need to be pushed flat by hand.

Arrange the sliced pears on top, then carefully cover the pears with the remaining cake mixture. Bake in the oven 45–55 minutes.

Allow the cake to cool in the pan. Dust with icing sugar and cut into wedges to serve.

This cake will keep for up to a week if stored in an airtight container in the refrigerator.

Serves 12

Note: If you cannot buy mixed spice, you can make your own by combining ½ teaspoon ground cinnamon, ¼ teaspoon ground ginger, a pinch of ground nutmeg and a pinch of ground cloves.

Where should I store chocolate?

Chocolate should be stored between 16 and 22°C (61–72°F) and protected from light and humidity. It should never be stored in a refrigerator, which causes chocolate to bloom or 'sweat', and even damages its capacity to melt properly.

Chocolate Upside-Down Cake

8 whole glacé (candied) cherries, halved
16 canned apricot halves, drained
125 g (4 oz) unsalted butter
1 cup (150 g, 5 oz) light soft brown sugar, lightly packed
2 large eggs
1½ cups (185 g, 6 oz) plain (all-purpose) flour, sifted
3 tablespoons cocoa powder, sifted
3 tablespoons drinking chocolate, sifted
1 teaspoon baking powder
½ cup (125 mL, 4 fl oz) milk
apricot jam, for glazing (optional)

Preheat the oven to 180°C (350°F). Lightly grease a 23 cm (9 in) springform cake pan and line the bottom with baking parchment.

Place a cherry half cut side up in each of the 16 apricot halves, then carefully place these cut side down in a pattern on the bottom of the lined cake pan.

Cream the butter and sugar until light and fluffy. Add the eggs one at a time, beating well after each addition. Now add the flour, cocoa, drinking chocolate and baking powder. When partly combined, add the milk and continue to mix until a smooth batter is formed.

Gently spread the mixture evenly over the apricot halves. Bake in the oven for 35 minutes or until the cake springs back when lightly touched.

As soon as the cake is baked, turn out of the pan, peel away the baking parchment and slide the cake upside down onto a serving plate. Serve immediately for the most compliments; otherwise, brush the top lightly with some boiled apricot jam, allow to cool and serve cold with a hot chocolate sauce.

This cake will keep for up to 2 days if stored in an airtight container in the refrigerator.

Serves 10–12

Deer's Back Torte

Chocolate Génoise

²/₃ cup (150 g, 5 oz) caster (superfine) sugar
8 large eggs
1 cup (125 g, 4 oz) plain (all-purpose) flour
¼ cup (30 g, 1 oz) cocoa powder
30 g (1 oz) unsalted butter, melted

Torte

250 g (8 oz) unsalted butter
1 cup (250 g, 8 oz) caster (superfine) sugar
60 g (2 oz) plus 500 g (1 lb) dark (plain or semisweet) chocolate, melted
9 large eggs, separated
310 g (10 oz) chocolate génoise, crumbled
1⅓ cups (150 g, 5 oz) ground almonds
½ cup (60 g, 2 oz) plain (all-purpose) flour
1 cup (125 g, 4 oz) flaked (sliced) almonds

To make the génoise, preheat the oven to 180°C (350°F). Lightly grease a 23 cm (9 in) springform cake pan and line the bottom with baking parchment. Beat the sugar and eggs for 10–12 minutes, or until ribbon stage is reached. Gently fold in half the flour and cocoa. Repeat the process with the remaining flour and cocoa, then fold in the butter.

Pour the mixture into the cake pan and bake 15–20 minutes. Allow the cake to cool for 5 minutes in the pan before turning out. Do not turn off the oven.

To make the torte, grease a semicircular or Balmoral cake pan, or a 20 x 10 x 10 cm (8 x 4 x 4 in) log pan.

Cream the butter and half of the caster sugar until light and fluffy. Beat in the 60 g (2 oz) dark chocolate, then add the egg yolks one at a time, beating well after each addition. Fold in the cake crumbs, ground almonds and flour.

In a separate bowl, whisk the egg whites until stiff peaks form, then gradually whisk in the remaining caster sugar. Continue whisking until all the sugar has dissolved.

Beat a little egg white mixture into the cake batter, then carefully fold in the remaining egg white mixture. Pour the batter into the cake pan and bake in the oven for 35–40 minutes, or until a metal skewer inserted into the top of the cake comes out clean.

Allow the cake to cool in the pan for 5 minutes before turning out onto a wire rack. Spike the cooled cake with the flaked almonds.

Slide a baking sheet under the wire rack and pour the 500 g (1 lb) dark chocolate over the top of the cake. Allow to set before serving.

Serves 10–12

Dobos Torte

Torte

8 large eggs, separated

1½ cups (250 g, 8 oz) icing (confectioners') sugar

1½ cups (185 g, 6 oz) plain (all-purpose) flour

Filling

250 g (8 oz) unsalted butter

⅔ cup (75 g, 2½ oz) cocoa powder

125 g (4 oz) dark (plain or semisweet) chocolate, melted

75 g (2½ oz) cornflour (cornstarch)

2¼ cups (560 mL, 18 fl oz) milk

5 large egg yolks

1½ cups (310 g, 10 oz) caster (superfine) sugar

Topping

1 cup (225 g, 7 oz) caster (superfine) sugar

30 g (1 oz) unsalted butter

toasted flaked (sliced) almonds, for decorating

To make the torte, preheat the oven to 180°C (350°F). Line five baking sheets with baking parchment and draw a 23 cm (9 in) circle on each sheet of parchment.

Beat the egg yolks and ¾ cup (125 g, 4 oz) of the icing sugar until thick and fluffy, about 20 minutes.

In a separate bowl, whisk the egg whites until stiff peaks form, then whisk in the remaining ¾ cup (125 g, 4 oz) icing sugar a spoonful at a time.

Very gently fold the flour and the egg whites into the egg yolk mixture.

Divide the mixture between the five circles and bake in the oven for 5–8 minutes or until springy to the touch. Cool on wire racks.

To make the filling, cream the butter until light and fluffy, and almost white. Beat in the cocoa powder and dark chocolate. Set aside.

Blend ½ cup (125 mL, 4 fl oz) of the milk, egg yolks and cornflour in a small bowl. Bring the remaining 1¾ cups (435 mL, 14 fl oz) milk to the boil in a saucepan. Stir in the caster sugar and then the egg yolk mixture, stirring all the time. Continue to stir over the heat and cook for 2 minutes, until thickened.

Remove from the heat and allow to cool. When completely cold, beat into the chocolate mixture. Set aside.

To make the topping, place the caster sugar in a saucepan and heat until it melts and caramelises, stirring occasionally. Add the butter and stir until melted and combined.

Pour the topping onto one of the cakes. Spread the caramel evenly and, while still soft, cut into 12 equal wedges with a hot, oiled, sharp knife.

To assemble the torte, spread the chocolate filling over the remaining cakes, leaving enough filling to cover the sides. Stack the cakes one on top of the other, then cover the sides of the torte with the remaining filling. Place the caramelised cake wedges on top of that.

Press the flaked almonds around the sides of the torte and serve.

Can be stored in an airtight container in the refrigerator for 3–4 days.

Serves 8–10

Note: The caramel topping may begin to break down to syrup after 2–3 days.

Great Moments in Chocolate

1875 After eight years of experimentation, Daniel Peter, of Switzerland, uses Henri Nestlé's condensed milk to create the first milk chocolate.

Dual Torte

¾ cup (90 g, 3 oz) flaked (sliced) almonds

Chocolate Torte

2 egg whites

¼ cup (60 g, 2 oz) caster (superfine) sugar

½ cup (90 g, 3 oz) icing (confectioners') sugar

1¼ cups (125 g, 4 oz) ground almonds

¼ cup (30 g, 1 oz) cocoa powder

White Torte

¾ cup (90 g, 3 oz) plain (all-purpose) flour

⅛ teaspoon baking powder

125 g (4 oz) butter

½ cup (125 g, 4 oz) caster (superfine) sugar

1¼ cups (125 g, 4 oz) ground almonds

2 large eggs

1 egg yolk (extra)

Preheat the oven to 180°C (350°F). Grease a 20 x 10 x 5 cm (8 x 4 x 2½ in) loaf pan with butter. Line the bottom of the pan with the flaked almonds.

To make the chocolate torte, whisk the egg white until stiff peaks form, then gradually beat in the caster sugar until dissolved. Fold in the icing sugar, ground almonds and cocoa powder.

Carefully pour the batter over the flaked almonds, spreading it around the sides of the pan. Set aside while you make the white torte.

Sift the flour and baking powder together. Cream the butter, caster sugar and ground almonds until light and fluffy. Add the eggs one at a time, including the extra egg yolk, beating well after each addition. Fold in the sifted flour.

Pour the white torte batter into the centre of the pan, into the well made by the chocolate torte batter. Bake for 35–40 minutes or until the cake springs back to the touch.

Allow the cake to cool for 5 minutes in the pan before turning out.

This torte will keep for up to a week in an airtight container in the refrigerator.

Serves 12

Fantasia Torte

Vanilla Sponge

4 large eggs, separated

a level $1/2$ cup (100g, $3^1/2$ oz) caster (superfine) sugar

3/4 cup (90 g, 3 oz) plain (all-purpose) flour

Chocolate Sponge

4 large eggs, separated

a level $1/2$ cup (100 g, $3^1/2$ oz) caster (superfine) sugar

$1/2$ cup (60 g, 2 oz) plain (all-purpose) flour

1/4 cup (30 g, 1 oz) cocoa powder

Milk Chocolate Marquise Filling

2 teaspoons powdered gelatin

1 tablespoon water

$1^1/2$ tablespoons liquid glucose

2 large egg yolks

250 g (8 oz) milk chocolate

$2^1/2$ cups (625 mL, 1 imp. pint) double (heavy, thickened) cream,
very lightly whipped

finely grated zest and juice of 1 orange

1 tablespoon Grand Marnier

For decoration

$2/3$ cup (225 g, 7 oz) apricot jam

marzipan roses

chocolate butterfly

Preheat the oven to 180°C (350°F). Lightly grease a baking sheet and line with baking parchment.

To make the vanilla sponge, whisk the egg yolks with half of the caster sugar until light and fluffy.

In a separate bowl, whisk the egg whites until stiff peaks form, then gradually whisk in the remaining caster sugar. Continue whisking until all the sugar has dissolved.

Gently fold together the two egg mixtures. Gently fold the flour into the eggs until well combined.

Make the chocolate sponge exactly as above, but sift the cocoa and flour together before folding into the egg mixture.

Using separate piping bags with 1 cm ($3/8$ in) nozzles, pipe alternate rows of the vanilla and chocolate sponge batters so that they touch and all the mixture is used. Bake in the oven for 12 minutes, or until very light golden brown on top.

Immediately invert the sponge onto a damp kitchen cloth and remove the baking parchment. Quickly cut a circular base from to fit a 20 cm (8 in) round cake pan. Cut strips of sponge to fit the depth of the pan and line the sides of the pan, making sure a tight seal is made.

To make the marquise filling, soak the gelatin in the water. Gently heat the glucose and gelatin in a saucepan until melted. Add the egg yolks to the gelatin mixture, then stir in the milk chocolate.

Add the warm chocolate mixture immediately to the cream, stirring as you do so, then add the orange juice and zest, and Grand Marnier. Pour into the sponge-lined pan and freeze for 1½ hours.

Bring the apricot jam and 1 tablespoon water to the boil and boil for 2 minutes. Brush the hot jam over the sides and the top of the frozen cake. Chill in the refrigerator for 30 minutes before decorating with the marzipan roses and chocolate butterfly. Serve.

This torte will keep for up to a week in an airtight container in the refrigerator.

Serves 10–12

Chocolate Pioneers
Christopher Columbus

Born in the port city of Genoa, Italy, in 1451, Columbus became a seaman and developed a passion to prove that India could be reached by sailing westwards. After elaborating this theory to King Ferdinand and Queen Isabella of Spain, he secured their backing for a voyage of discovery in a fleet of three ships, the *Nino*, *Pinto* and *Santa Maria*, and in 1492 he became the first European to reach the Americas. There were three subsequent voyages and on the last expedition, in 1502, in what is now Nicaragua, he encountered people using cocoa beans as a form of currency and the base ingredient of drinking chocolate. Although he returned to Spain with cocoa beans, they were of poor quality and Columbus failed to understand the true value and potential of cocoa. His version of drinking chocolate found little favour in the Spanish court.

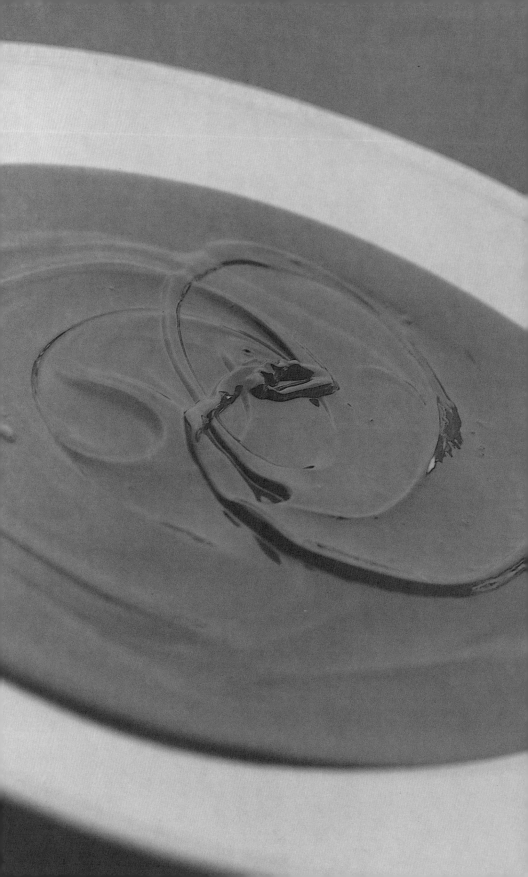

Dip Me in the Language of Chocolate

The chocaholic abroad is often able to sniff out the closest source of chocolate, and like a bee to nectar veer straight towards the appropriate shop or store. In a foreign-language country, it is usually possible to gesture or point towards the object of addiction; but if you are ever in dire need of the correct terminology, you can always consult the following list to find words for cocoa and chocolate in an appropriate language.

Language	Cocoa Powder	Chocolate
Belgian/Flemish	cacao	chocolade
Czech	kakao	cokolade
Danish	kakao or kakaobonne	Chokolade or chokoladebrun
Dutch	cacao	chocolaatje or chocolade
English	cocoa	chocolate
Estonian	kakao	shokolade
Finnish	kaakao	suklaa
French	cacao	chocolat
German	cacao	Schokolade
Hungarian	kakao	csokolade
Italian	cacao	cioccolata
Lithuanian	kakao	sokolade
Norwegian	kakao	sjokolade
Polish	kakao	czekolada
Portugese	cacao	chocolate
Rumanian	cacao	ciocolata
Spanish	cacao	chocolate
Swedish	kakao	choklad

Featherlight Gâteau

125 g (4 oz) unsalted butter
250 g (8 oz) dark (plain or semisweet) chocolate, chopped
6 large eggs, separated
a level $\frac{1}{3}$ cup (75 g, 2$\frac{1}{2}$ oz) caster (superfine) sugar
1$\frac{1}{2}$ tablespoons plain (all-purpose) flour
24 chocolate squares
cocoa powder, for dusting

Preheat the oven to 180°C (350°F). Grease and lightly flour a 23 cm (9 in) springform cake pan.

Melt the butter and chopped chocolate in the top of a double boiler, stirring to combine.

Whisk the egg yolks and caster sugar until thick and pale. Fold in the melted chocolate mixture until well combined. Gently fold in the flour.

In a separate bowl, whisk the egg whites until stiff peaks form and then gently fold through the egg yolk mixture.

Pour three-quarters of the cake batter into the prepared pan and bake in the oven for 40 minutes. Reserve the remaining batter.

When baked, the cake should have shrunk slightly from the sides of the pan. Allow it to cool in the pan — it should sink in the middle as it cools.

When completely cool, remove the sides of the pan from the cake and pour the reserved cake batter into the hollow on top of the cake. Take a little of the batter and spread it thinly around the sides of the cake, spreading the remainder evenly over the top.

Place the cake onto a plate or serving dish, and then begin arranging the chocolate squares around the sides, making certain that each one overlaps another. Cut the remaining squares into triangles and insert upright into the top of the cake.

Refrigerate for 1 hour, then remove and dust with the cocoa powder before cutting with a hot knife to serve.

Can be stored in an airtight container in the refrigerator for 4–5 days.

Serves 12

Heavy Flourless Chocolate Cake

310 g (10 oz) dark chocolate
150 g (5 oz) unsalted butter
¾ cup (185 g, 6 oz) sugar
6 large eggs, separated
¼ cup (60 mL, 2 fl oz) Grand Marnier
softly whipped fresh cream, to serve
strands of crystallised orange zest, to serve
icing (confectioners') sugar, to serve

Preheat the oven to 160°C (325°F). Grease a 23 cm (9 in) springform cake pan, lining the bottom and sides with baking parchment or silicon paper.

Melt the chocolate with the butter, stirring until smooth.

Beat the egg yolks with three-quarters of the sugar until thick. Slowly beat in the Grand Marnier.

In a separate bowl, whisk the egg whites until stiff peaks form. Slowly add the remaining sugar, whisking until the sugar has dissolved.

Add the melted chocolate mixture to egg yolk mixture, then slowly and carefully fold in the egg whites.

Pour the batter into the cake pan and bake for 1 hour. Reduce the oven temperature to 150°C (300°F) and bake for a further 30 minutes.

Turn off the heat and leave the cake in the oven to cool. The cake should 'fall' or sink 4–5 cm (1¾–2 in) in height.

When the cake is at room temperature, serve slices of cake with softly whipped cream and 2–3 strands of fresh crystallised orange zest. Lightly dust the side of the plate without cream with icing sugar.

Can be stored in an airtight container in the refrigerator for 5–6 days.

Serves 8–10

Great Moments in Chocolate

1879 Rodolphe Lindt, a Swiss chocolate manufacturer, invents 'conching', a method of smoothing chocolate which has given us that melting quality and taste which we know and love today.

Light Flourless Chocolate Cake

625 g (1¼ lb) dark (plain or bittersweet) chocolate
500g (1 lb) unsalted butter
12 large eggs, separated
1¾ cups (375g, 12 oz) plus ⅔ cup (150 g, 5 oz) caster (superfine) sugar
2¼ cups (250g, 8 oz) ground almonds
1 teaspoon Grand Marnier
1 teaspoon instant coffee granules
icing (confectioners') sugar, for dusting

Preheat the oven to 180°C (350°F). Line the bottom of a 23 cm (9 in) springform cake pan with baking parchment and grease the sides well with butter.

Melt the chocolate with the butter over a double boiler, stirring until melted and combined.

Remove from the heat. Stir in the egg yolks, the 1¾ cups (375 g, 12 oz) caster sugar and the almond meal. Combine the Grand Marnier with the instant coffee. Stir into the chocolate mixture. Set aside.

In a large, clean bowl, whisk the egg whites until light, stiff peaks form. Continue whisking slowly, adding the ⅔ cup (150 g, 5 oz) caster sugar a little at a time until it is all incorporated and dissolved.

Slowly fold the egg whites into the chocolate mixture, then pour the batter into the prepared cake pan.

Bake in the oven for 50–60 minutes, or until a small skewer inserted into the cake comes out clean. Allow the cake to cool in the pan before turning out. Dust with icing sugar to serve.

Can be stored in an airtight container in the refrigerator for 5–6 days.

Serves 8–10

Note: This cake will 'souffle', meaning that it will rise during cooking and then sink during cooling. This is a normal process for egg-white raised products.

Great Moments in Chocolate

1893 An 11-metre-tall, 12-tonne chocolate sculpture, the 'Statue of Germania', is produced for the Columbian Exposition in Chicago by the Stollwerck Chocolate Company of Germany.

L'ecstasy
Mousse Cake

Chocolate Sponge

$\frac{1}{3}$ cup (45 g, 1$\frac{1}{2}$ oz) plain (all-purpose) flour, sifted

$\frac{1}{4}$ cup (30 g, 1 oz) cocoa powder, sifted

$\frac{1}{4}$ teaspoon baking powder

$\frac{1}{4}$ cup (60 g, 2 oz) plus 2 tablespoons granulated sugar

4 large egg yolks

2 large egg whites

3 tablespoons vegetable oil

2 teaspoons water

Dark Chocolate Mousse

$\frac{1}{2}$ cup (125 mL, 4 fl oz) milk

250 g (8 oz) dark (plain or bittersweet) chocolate, chopped

1 tablespoon vegetable oil

$\frac{3}{4}$ cup (185 mL, 6 fl oz) double (heavy, thickened) cream

finely grated zest of 1 orange

Orange Syrup

a level $\frac{1}{2}$ cup (100 mL, 3$\frac{1}{2}$ fl oz) water

$\frac{1}{2}$ cup (125 g, 4 oz) caster (superfine) sugar

finely grated zest and juice of 1 orange

1$\frac{1}{2}$ tablespoons Grand Marnier

White Chocolate Mousse

1 teaspoon powdered gelatin

2 tablespoons water

$\frac{1}{2}$ cup (125 mL, 4 fl oz) milk

250 g (8 oz) white chocolate, chopped

1 teaspoon ground cinnamon

1 tablespoon vegetable oil

$\frac{3}{4}$ cup (185 mL, 6 fl oz) double (heavy, thickened) cream

Ganache

125 g (4 oz) dark (plain or semisweet) chocolate, chopped

$\frac{1}{2}$ cup (125 mL, 4 fl oz) single (light) cream

Preheat the oven to 180°C (350°F). Lightly grease a 23 cm (9 in) springform cake pan and line the bottom with baking parchment.

To make the chocolate sponge, sift together the flour, cocoa powder and baking powder. Set aside. Whisk the egg yolks and the $\frac{1}{4}$ cup (60 g, 2 oz)

95

granulated sugar until the mixture is stiff and pale, and forms a ribbon.

In a separate bowl, whisk the egg whites until stiff peaks form. Slowly add the 2 tablespoons sugar, whisking continuously until all the sugar has dissolved. Add to the egg yolk mixture and re-sift the dry ingredients over the top of both. Gently fold the mixture until thoroughly combined.

Spread into the prepared cake pan and bake in the oven for 25–30 minutes. When baked — the sponge will only be about 4–5 cm (1¾–2 in) high — remove from the pan and cool on a wire rack.

To make the dark chocolate mousse, bring the milk slowly to the boil in a heavy-based saucepan. Remove from the heat and add the dark chocolate. Stir in the oil and orange zest, and continue stirring until smooth. Allow the chocolate mixture to cool to lukewarm.

Whip the cream into stiff peaks, then fold in the chocolate mixture. Cover the mousse with cling film (plastic wrap) and refrigerate until firm enough to spread.

To make the orange syrup, bring the water and caster sugar slowly to the boil in a saucepan. Remove from the heat when the sugar has dissolved. Stir in the orange juice and zest, and the Grand Marnier. Allow to cool.

To assemble, cut the sponge into two layers and place the first half, cut side down, onto a cake board or platter. Using a pastry brush, brush the top of the sponge with a little of the orange syrup. Reserve the remaining syrup.

Spread the dark chocolate mousse onto the centre of the sponge so that it covers the top of the layer entirely, but is domed in the middle.

Enclose the mousse-covered sponge layer with the ring of a clean springform pan and close it tightly around the cake. Refrigerate until the white chocolate mousse is ready.

To make the white chocolate mousse, sprinkle the gelatine powder over the water and allow to soak. Bring the milk slowly to the boil in a saucepan. Add the soaked gelatine to the boiled milk and stir to dissolve. Remove from the heat and add the white chocolate and cinnamon. Stir in the oil and continue stirring until smooth. Allow the chocolate mixture to cool to lukewarm.

Whip the cream into stiff peaks, then fold in the chocolate mixture. Cover the mousse with cling film (plastic wrap) and refrigerate until firm enough to spread.

Take the chocolate mousse-covered sponge layer from the refrigerator and spread the white chocolate mousse evenly over the domed dark chocolate mousse, levelling off the top and filling the gap between the top of the chocolate mousse and the side of the springform ring.

Place the second layer of sponge on top of the white chocolate mousse and press down slightly so that the mousse comes up around the side of the cake and is almost level with its top.

Brush the top of the cake with the reserved orange syrup and refrigerate overnight. (It may also be frozen for up to 2 weeks at this stage.)

To make the ganache, bring the cream to the boil in a heavy-based saucepan. Remove from the heat and add the chocolate. Allow to sit for several minutes before stirring to a smooth consistency. Cool to lukewarm.

Remove the cake from the refrigerator and pour the ganache over the top. Spread evenly and refrigerate for 30–40 minutes or until the ganache is firm.

To serve, remove the cake from refrigerator and run a knife around the inside edge of the cake pan. Remove the springform ring and serve the cake whole on a serving plate or in thin slices.

Serves 10–12

Great Moments in Chocolate

1907 The Hershey company releases the Hershey Kiss.

Men's Torte

Chocolate Génoise

⅔ cup (150 g, 5 oz) caster (superfine) sugar
8 large eggs
1 cup (125 g, 4 oz) plain (all-purpose) flour, sifted
¼ cup (30 g, 1 oz) cocoa powder, sifted
30 g (1 oz) unsalted butter, melted

Filling

2½ cups (625 mL, 1 imp. pint) dry white wine
¾ cup (185 g, 6 oz) granulated sugar
⅔ cup (90 g, 3 oz) custard powder
½ cup (125 mL, 4 fl oz) water
3 large eggs, lightly beaten

To Decorate

250 g (8 oz) marzipan
225 g (7 oz) dark (plain or semisweet) chocolate, melted
12 maraschino cherries
1 cup (125 g, 4 oz) flaked (sliced) almonds, toasted

Preheat the oven to 180°C (350°F). Lightly grease a 23 cm (9 in) springform cake pan and line the bottom with baking parchment.

To make the chocolate génoise, beat the caster sugar and eggs until ribbon stage is reached, about 10–12 minutes. Gently fold in half the flour and cocoa. Repeat the process with the remaining flour and cocoa, then fold in the butter.

Pour into the springform pan and bake in the oven for 15–20 minutes. Allow to cool in the pan for 5 minutes before turning out onto a wire rack.

Line the bottom and sides of a clean 23 cm (9 in) springform pan with baking parchment. Slice the sponge into four layers horizontally and place the top layer into the prepared pan.

To make the filling, bring the wine and granulated sugar to the boil in a saucepan. Blend the custard powder and water in a small bowl, then stir into the lightly beaten eggs. Pour in the hot wine syrup, beating all the time. Return the mixture to the saucepan and, stirring continuously, heat until the custard boils and thickens.

Pour one-third of the custard on top of the sponge layer in the springform pan and top with another layer of sponge. Repeat this process twice with the remaining custard and layers of sponge. Press down lightly to spread the filling evenly, then chill in the refrigerator for 2 hours.

To decorate, roll the marzipan into a 23 cm (9 in) circle and cover with the dark chocolate. Using a hot knife, cut the circle into 12 wedges.

Remove the cake from the refrigerator and cut into 12 wedges. Top each with a marzipan wedge tilted on its side, supporting each wedge with a maraschino cherry (see picture). Press the flaked almonds around the side of the torte and serve.

Can be stored in an airtight container in the refrigerator for 3–4 days.

Serves 8–12

Can I add liquids to chocolate?

Small amounts of most liquids can spoil chocolate. Fat-based liquids such as cream, egg yolks, butter, oil and copha (coconut oil) can be heated with chocolate, and chocolate can be melted with a small amount of liquid such as cream and alcohol. As a general rule, chocolate can be mixed with a water-based liquid if the chocolate is smaller in quantity than the liquid.

Pithiviers

500 g (1 lb) puff pastry

Filling

100 g (3½ oz) unsalted butter

2 tablespoons cocoa powder

a level ½ cup (100 g, 3½ oz) caster (superfine) sugar

1 large egg yolk

¼ cup (30 g, 1 oz) plain (all-purpose) flour, sifted

1 cup (100 g, 3½ oz) ground almonds

beaten egg wash*

apricot glaze**

½ cup (60 g, 2 oz) flaked (sliced) almonds, toasted

Preheat the oven to 180°C (350°F). Line a baking sheet with baking parchment.

Roll out the pastry and cut two 23 cm (9 in) circles. Chill while preparing the filling.

To make the filling, cream the butter, cocoa powder and sugar until light and fluffy. Add the egg yolk and beat for 3 minutes. Beat in the flour and ground almonds.

Place the pastry circles on the prepared sheet and brush a 4 cm (1¾ in) border of egg wash around the edge of the pastry circle.

Place the filling in the centre, keeping it inside the egg-wash border, and shape it into a mound 2 cm (¾ in) high in the middle.

Top with the second pastry circle. Crimp around the edge with the fingertips. Using a small, sharp knife, lightly mark lines on the top of the pastry. Brush with beaten egg wash.

Bake in the oven for 40 minutes or until both the bottom and top are cooked. While still hot, brush with apricot glaze. Allow the glaze to cool and then sprinkle with flaked almonds. Place the baking sheet on a wire rack and allow to cool before serving.

This cake will last for up to 2 days if stored in an airtight container.

Serves 10

*Egg wash gives a glossy sheen to cakes and is also used to join and seal layers of pastry before baking. To make egg wash, lightly beat 1 large egg and mix in 30 mL (1 fl oz) water. It is now ready to use. Egg wash can be stored in a covered container in the refrigerator for up to 2 days.

** To make the apricot glaze, place 250 g (9 oz) apricot jam, 60 ml (2 fl oz) water and 2 teaspoons lemon juice in a saucepan and stir until smooth. Boil for 10–15 minutes, then force through a fine wire strainer. Makes enough to cover one 23 cm (9 in) cake. Leftover glaze can be stored for up to 3 weeks in an airtight container in the refrigerator.

Pyramid of Dreams

6 large eggs

⅔ cup (150 g, 5 oz) caster (superfine) sugar

1 cup (125 g, 4 oz) plain (all-purpose) flour, sifted

3 tablespoons cocoa powder, sifted

1 cup (250 mL, 8 fl oz) double (heavy, thickened) cream

½ cup (125 mL, 4 fl oz) plus 2½ tablespoons orange liqueur *or* freshly
squeezed orange juice

500 g (1 lb) white chocolate, chopped

drinking chocolate, for dusting

Preheat the oven to 180°C (350°F). Lightly grease three 28 x 18 cm
(11 x 7 in) baking pans and line each pan with baking parchment.

Using an electric mixer on the highest setting, whisk the eggs and sugar until
very thick and frothy. Lightly sprinkle the flour and cocoa over the mixture and
fold in very gently by hand. Divide the mixture evenly between the three pans
and, using a spatula or palette knife, evenly spread to the edges of each pan.

Bake in the oven for 15–20 minutes, or until the sponge has shrunk slightly
from the sides of the pan. Allow to cool in the pans for 5 minutes before
turning out onto wire racks to cool completely.

To make the chocolate filling, bring the cream and the 2½ tablespoons
orange liqueur to the boil in a saucepan. Remove from the heat and add the
white chocolate. Stir until the chocolate has melted. Pour the filling into a dish
and chill in the refrigerator, stirring from time to time. Do not allow the filling
to become too thick; it must remain of spreading consistency.

Trim the edges off each sponge along the longest sides, then cut each sponge
in half again along the longest length. Sprinkle each strip of sponge with the
½ cup (125 mL, 4 fl oz) orange liqueur.

Thinly spread the chocolate filling on top of each sponge strip, leaving the top
strip plain, then stack the strips on top of the other. Chill the stack in the
refrigerator for 30 minutes. Reserve the rest of the chocolate filling.

Place the chilled cake lengthwise on the edge of a bench top. Place a ruler
along the top edge of the cake furthest from you and cut diagonally through
to the bottom edge nearest you with a clean knife. The ruler and bench top
are used to guide the knife. When cut, you will have two triangles of cake.

Stand the triangles so that the layers of cake run vertically. Join the 2 triangles
together with a thin layer of the reserved chocolate filling to make a pyramid
shape. Cover the sloping sides with the remaining chocolate filling and chill
for a further 30 minutes. Dust lightly with drinking chocolate before serving.

The Pyramid of Dreams will keep for 3–4 days in an airtight container in the
refrigerator.

Serves 12

Raspberry Fantasy

Crust

1 level cup (100 g, 3½ oz) plain (all-purpose) flour
100 g (3½ oz) unsalted butter, softened
1 teaspoon ground cinnamon
⅓ cup (45 g, 1½ oz) finely chopped almonds
¼ cup (45 g, 1½ oz) light soft brown sugar

Filling

150 g (5 oz) unsalted butter, softened
⅔ cup (150 g, 5 oz) caster (superfine) sugar
2 large eggs
100 g (3½ oz) white chocolate, melted
225 g (7 oz) fresh raspberries

To Decorate

extra fresh raspberries
chocolate curls

Preheat the oven to 180°C (350°F). Lightly grease a 23 cm (9 in) springform cake pan and line the bottom of the pan with baking parchment.

To make the crust, gently combine the flour, butter and cinnamon. Add the almonds and brown sugar, and mix until a soft paste has formed.

Press the mixture into the prepared pan and bake in the oven for 10 minutes, or until light golden brown. Allow to cool in the pan.

To make the filling, cream the butter and sugar together until light and fluffy. Add the eggs one at a time, beating well before adding the second egg. When combined, fold into the white chocolate.

Fold through the raspberries and pour the mixture directly on top of the cooled base. Refrigerate for 1 hour.

Decorate with extra fresh raspberries and chocolate curls, and serve immediately.

This will keep for up to a week in an airtight container in the refrigerator.

Serves 12

Sacher Torte

1 1/4 cups (150 g, 5 oz) plain (all-purpose) flour
1/3 cup (45 g, 1 1/2 oz) cocoa powder
185 g (6 oz) unsalted butter
1 cup (250 g, 8 oz) caster (superfine) sugar
7 large eggs, separated
1/3 cup (45 g, 1 1/2 oz) ground almonds
2 3/4 cups (300 g, 10 oz) ground hazelnuts
3/4 cup plus 2 tablespoons (310 g, 10 oz) apricot jam
300 g (10 oz) marzipan
375 g (12 oz) dark (plain or semisweet) chocolate, melted
60 g (2 oz) milk chocolate, melted

Preheat the oven to 180°C (350°F). Lightly grease a 23 cm (9 in) springform cake pan and line the bottom of the pan with baking parchment.

Mix the flour and cocoa powder together and sift twice.

Cream the butter and 1/3 cup (90 g 3 oz) of the caster sugar until light and fluffy. Gradually add the egg yolks, beating well after each addition.

Gently fold in the sifted flour and cocoa, almonds and hazelnuts by hand.

In a separate bowl, whisk the egg whites until stiff peaks form. Gradually whisk in the remaining 2/3 cup (150 g, 5 oz) caster sugar a spoonful at a time. Continue whisking until all the sugar has dissolved.

Take one-quarter of the beaten egg whites and gently mix into the stiff chocolate mixture by hand. Very carefully fold in the remaining egg whites.

Pour the mixture into the prepared pan and bake in the oven for 35–40 minutes, or until the top of the cake is firm to touch. Allow to cool in the pan for 5 minutes before turning out onto a wire cooling rack.

When cold, cut into four layers horizontally. Spread each layer thinly with the apricot jam, then stack the layers one on top of the other. Spread the remaining apricot jam over the top and sides of the cake.

On a lightly floured surface, roll the marzipan thinly enough so that it will cover the top and sides of the cake. Cover the cake with marzipan and trim away any excess.

Spread the dark chocolate over the top and sides of the cake using a warm palette knife. Make sure that the chocolate is completely smooth and free of bubbles. As the chocolate begins to set, use a large, hot knife to mark the chocolate into 12 segments so that it is easy to cut later.

When the chocolate has begun to set, use a small paper piping (pastry) bag filled with the milk chocolate to pipe the word 'Sacher' on each portion of the cake. Place the cake in the refrigerator until ready to serve.

This cake will keep for up to a week in an airtight container in the refrigerator.

Serves 12

Savoy Sponge

⅔ cup (75 g, 2½ oz) plain (all-purpose) flour
¼ cup (30 g, 1 oz) cocoa powder
¼ teaspoon baking powder
pinch of salt
1 level cup (225 g, 7 oz) sugar
4 large eggs, separated
1 egg yolk

Preheat the oven to 180°C (375°F). Lightly grease a 23 cm (9 in) springform cake pan and line the bottom of the pan with baking parchment.

Sift the flour, cocoa, baking powder and salt into a bowl.

Whisk together ⅔ cup (150 g, 5 oz) of the sugar and the egg yolks for 4–5 minutes until stiff and pale, and forming a ribbon.

In a separate bowl, whisk the egg whites until stiff peaks form. Gradually whisk in the remaining ¼ cup (60 g, 2 oz) sugar. Continue whisking until all the sugar has dissolved.

Fold the egg whites into the egg yolk mixture, then gently fold in the flour mixture.

Spread the batter in the prepared pan and bake in the oven for 35–40 minutes. Remove the cake from the pan and cool on a wire rack.

This sponge will keep for 4–5 days if stored in an airtight container.

Serves 8

Note: This sponge can be used as a base for cream cakes or for recipes requiring sponge crumbs. It is delicious and light on its own or spread with jam (jelly).

Chocolate Pioneers
Antonio Carletti

In 1606, Antonio Carletti returned to Italy from the West Indies with the secret of the cocoa drink, which the Spaniards had monopolised for a century. From Italy, drinking chocolate spread throughout Europe.

Wine, Oil and Cocoa Sponge

1 cup (125 g, 4 oz) plain (all-purpose) flour

2 tablespoons cocoa powder

1/4 teaspoon salt

5 large eggs, separated

1 level cup (225 g, 7 oz) granulated sugar

3 teaspoons finely grated orange zest

3 teaspoons finely grated lemon zest

1/3 cup (90 mL, 3 fl oz) olive oil

1/3 cup (90 mL, 3 fl oz) sweet white wine

2 large egg whites (extra)

1/2 teaspoon cream of tartar

icing (confectioners') sugar, to serve

Preheat the oven to 180°C (350°F). Grease a 20 cm (8 in) springform cake pan and line it with baking parchment paper, leaving a deep collar around side of the pan for rising.

Sift the flour, cocoa powder and salt together. Beat the egg yolks and half of the granulated sugar in an electric mixer until thick and pale. Add the orange and lemon zest, olive oil and wine, and beat until combined.

In a separate bowl, whisk the egg whites (including the extra whites) with the cream of tartar until soft peaks form. Gradually whisk in the remaining granulated sugar and beat until the egg whites hold stiff peaks and the sugar has dissolved.

Gradually fold the egg whites into the egg yolk mixture at the same time as sprinkling the sifted cocoa and flour over the top of the mixture. Fold through gently with a metal spoon until the egg whites and dry ingredients are thoroughly incorporated.

Pour the mixture into the prepared pan — do not smooth with a knife. Bake in the middle of the oven for 20 minutes.

Lower the temperature to 150°C (300°F) and bake for a further 35–40 minutes.

Turn off the oven and place a sheet of buttered baking parchment on top of the cake. Leave the cake in the oven for a further 10 minutes.

Remove the cake from the oven and cool in the pan on a wire rack. When cool, carefully turn out of the pan and dust with icing sugar before serving.

This cake will keep for 4–5 days in an airtight container.

Serves 10–12

Boiled Chocolate Glaze

a level 1⅓ cups (280 g, 9 oz) caster (superfine) sugar
225 g (7 oz) dark (plain or semisweet) chocolate, chopped
⅔ cup (150 mL, 5 fl oz) water

Place all the ingredients into a saucepan and slowly bring to the boil, stirring continuously. Allow to boil for 6 minutes, making sure that the mixture does not catch on the bottom.

Cool the glaze slightly before pouring over glazed or marzipan-covered cakes. Refrigerate the cake until the glaze is firm before cutting.

Makes enough to cover one 23 cm (9 in) cake

Chocolate Buttercream

310 g (10 oz) unsalted butter, softened
1 cup (150 g, 5 oz) icing (confectioners') sugar, sifted
2 large eggs
100 g (3½ oz) dark (plain or semisweet) chocolate, melted
1 teaspoon vanilla essence (extract)

Cream the butter and icing sugar until light, fluffy and pale. Add the eggs one at a time, beating well after each addition.

Add the melted chocolate and stir in quickly before the chocolate sets or becomes hard.

Lastly, add the vanilla essence and continue beating for a further 10 minutes at medium speed, until the mixture is light and creamy.

Makes enough to cover one 23 cm (9 in) cake

Great Moments in Chocolate

1915 In Adelaide, South Australia, Alf Haigh launches Haigh's Chocolates — destined to become Australia's longest lasting family-owned chocolate company.

Chocolate Frosting

6 tablespoons cocoa powder, sifted
3 cups (500 g, 16 oz) icing (confectioners') sugar, sifted
1 $\frac{1}{2}$ tablespoons liquid glucose
75 g (2 $\frac{1}{2}$ oz) unsalted butter, softened
2 $\frac{1}{2}$ tablespoons water

Using an electric mixer, slowly blend the cocoa, icing sugar, liquid glucose and butter in a mixing bowl.

When combined, slowly add the water, beating all the time.

When the ingredients are completely combined, beat the mixture for a further 15 minutes until the frosting is light and fluffy.

Makes enough to cover one 23 cm (9 in) cake

Ganache

$\frac{2}{3}$ cup (150 mL, 5 fl oz) double (heavy, thickened) cream
30 g (1 oz) unsalted butter
500 g (1 lb) dark (plain or semisweet) chocolate, chopped

Bring the cream and butter slowly to the boil in a saucepan.

Add the dark chocolate to the boiling liquid, then remove the pan from the heat. Stir until all the chocolate has melted and the mixture is thick and smooth.

Use immediately.

Makes enough to cover one 23 cm (9 in) cake

Chocolate Water Icing

1 1/2 cups (250 g, 8 oz) icing (confectioners') sugar

3 tablespoons cocoa powder

1/4 cup (60 mL, 2 fl oz) boiling water

Sift the icing sugar and cocoa into a bowl.

Stir in the boiling water a little at a time, firstly to make a stiff paste and then to thin it down to the required thickness.

Spread onto slices or cakes using a warm, wet knife to give a smooth finish.

Makes enough to cover one 23 cm (9 in) cake

Why is my chocolate covered in a white-grey film?

This effect, called 'bloom', is due to unintended heating and cooling, such as a transition from a hot car to an air-conditioned room, a variation that brings the cocoa butter to the surface. The chocolate is still quite edible, but would require re-tempering to return to normal. Of course, this is not an option with individual chocolates.

White Butter
Delight

½ cup (125 mL, 4 fl oz) milk
125 g (4 oz) white chocolate buttons
¼ cup (60 g, 2 oz) caster (superfine) sugar
1 large egg yolk
125 g (4 oz) butter, softened to room temperature

Bring the milk slowly to the boil in a saucepan.

Remove from the heat and immediately add the white chocolate, stirring until melted, then add the caster sugar and continue stirring until it is dissolved. Add the egg yolk and stir well until combined. Allow the mixture to cool to room temperature (almost cold).

Using a wooden spoon, stir the chocolate mixture into the butter in three or four batches, stirring only until the mixture is just combined each time. When all of the chocolate mixture has been stirred through, allow the mixture to stand for 5 minutes before using.

Makes enough to cover one 23 cm (9 in) cake

Wicked Chocolate Cream

1 level cup (225 mL, 7 fl oz) double (heavy, thickened) cream
60 g (2 oz) unsalted butter
2 tablespoons icing (confectioners') sugar, sifted
125 g (4 oz) milk chocolate, chopped

Bring the cream and butter slowly to the boil in a saucepan. Remove pan from the heat and add the remaining ingredients. Stir until combined.

Refrigerate the chocolate cream until cold. Whisk until stiff and use immediately.

Makes enough to cover one 23 cm (9 in) cake

Ganache Soufflé
or Whipped Ganache

1 level cup (225 mL, 7 fl oz) double (heavy, thickened) cream
60 g (2 oz) unsalted butter
500 g (1 lb) milk chocolate, chopped

Bring the cream and butter slowly to the boil in a saucepan. Remove the pan from the heat and quickly stir in the milk chocolate. Continue stirring until the chocolate has melted and the mixture is thick and smooth.

Allow the ganache to cool to room temperature and then place in the refrigerator. Stir every 5 minutes until it becomes quite thick and hard to stir.

Beat the ganache with an electric mixer until it has increased in volume and lightened in colour quite considerably. (If the mixture looks as if it may curdle at any stage, place the bowl into a pot of warm water and allow the mixture to melt slightly before continuing to whip with the electric mixer.)

Use immediately.

Makes enough to cover one 23 cm (9 in) cake

Great Moments
in Chocolate

1923 Brown and Haley launch a log-shaped, crunchie candy coated with chocolate and diced almond, which a local librarian dubs the 'Almond Roca'. She also suggests an ancient Sevillian coat of arms as a logo.

Liberty consists in doing
what one desires.

John Stuart Mills
On Liberty

parting
pleasures

desserts

Baked Chocolate Cheesecake

Base

200 g (7 oz) shortbread cookie crumbs

5 teaspoons caster (superfine) sugar

3 tablespoons cocoa powder

60 g (2 oz) unsalted butter, melted

Filling

650 g (21 oz) cream cheese

1 1/4 cups (250 g, 8 oz) caster (superfine) sugar

250 g (8 oz) dark (plain or semisweet) chocolate, melted

90 g (3 oz) white chocolate, melted

2 large eggs

2 tablespoons double (heavy, thickened) cream

1/3 cup (90 mL, 3 fl oz) sour cream

3 tablespoons instant coffee granules, mixed with
2 tablespoons hot water

Preheat the oven to 160°C (325°F). Lightly grease a 23 cm (9 in) springform cake pan and line the bottom with baking parchment.

To make the base, place the cookie crumbs, caster sugar and cocoa powder into a bowl. Pour over the butter and stir until all the ingredients are combined. Spread the mixture over the bottom of the prepared pan and press the crumb base flat with the back of a spoon. Set aside.

To make the filling, whip the cream cheese with the caster sugar until smooth and free of lumps. Add the dark and white chocolates, and continue whipping so that no lumps of chocolate form.

Add the eggs one at a time, beating well after each addition. When the eggs are combined, scrape down the sides of the bowl. Add the cream, sour cream and instant coffee, and continue beating until thoroughly combined.

Pour the mixture over the base and place the cheesecake in the oven. Bake for 55 minutes. Remove from the oven and allow to cool in the pan for 30 minutes.

Refrigerate, still in the pan, to ensure that the cheesecake is completely set. Remove from the springform pan and cut with a hot, damp knife to serve.

This cheesecake can be stored wrapped in cling film (plastic wrap) in the refrigerator for 4–5 days.

Makes 8–12 servings

Note: To maintain freshness, place a small sheet of wax (greaseproof) paper against the side of the cheesecake where a slice has been removed.

Chocolate Chip Cookie Dough Cheesecake

Cookie Dough

60 g (2 oz) unsalted butter

1 tablespoon soft brown sugar

1/4 cup (60 g, 2 oz) granulated sugar

1 tablespoon cold water

2 tablespoons plain (all-purpose) flour

185 g (6 oz) dark (plain or semisweet) chocolate, chopped or grated

Base

225 g (7 oz) chocolate cookie crumbs

1/4 cup (60 g, 2 oz) granulated sugar

3 tablespoons unsalted butter, melted

Filling

750 g (1 1/2 lb) cream cheese, softened

1 3/4 cups (435 mL, 14 fl oz) sweetened condensed milk

3 large eggs

Preheat the oven to 180°C (350°F). Lightly grease a 23 cm (9 in) springform cake pan and line the bottom with baking parchment.

To make the cookie dough, cream the butter and both sugars until light and fluffy.

Stir in the water, flour and dark chocolate. Mix until all the ingredients are combined. Refrigerate until firm.

To make the base, combine the chocolate cookie crumbs, granulated sugar and butter in a small bowl. When combined, spread over the bottom of the prepared pan and press the crumb base flat with the back of a spoon. Set aside.

To make the filling, beat the cream cheese until soft before adding the condensed milk and eggs. Continue beating until smooth and free of lumps. Pour the cream cheese mixture over the crumb base.

Take the cookie dough and place teaspoonfuls of the mixture over the top of the cream cheese filling. Lightly press the dough pieces below the surface of the filling.

Bake the cheesecake for 1 hour. Remove from the oven and allow to cool in the pan on a wire rack.

Refrigerate for 3–4 hours before cutting into thin slices and serving.

This cheesecake will keep for up to a week if stored in an airtight container in the refrigerator.

Makes 10–12 servings

Chocolate Crème Brûlée

3 cups (750 mL, 24 fl oz) double (heavy, thickened) cream
finely grated zest of 2 oranges
280 g (9 oz) dark (plain or semisweet) chocolate, finely chopped
7 large egg yolks
¼ cup (60 mL, 2 fl oz) Grand Marnier *or* other orange liqueur
⅓ cup (90 g, 3 oz) caster (superfine) sugar
400 g (13 oz) red berries (strawberries, raspberries, blackberries)
1 cup (250 mL, 10 fl oz) double (heavy, thickened) cream

Preheat the oven to 200°C (400°F).

Bring the cream and orange zest to the boil in a large, heavy-based saucepan. Once boiling, add the dark chocolate, then remove from the heat. Stir slowly until the chocolate has completely melted and the mixture is smooth.

Lightly whisk the egg yolks with the Grand Marnier until the yolks are just broken up and the mixture is combined. Slowly pour through a strainer in a clean bowl, and then divide the mixture between 6–8 soufflé ramekins.

Place the ramekins into a deep baking dish or roasting pan. Carefully fill the pan with cold water to halfway up the sides of the ramekins. Bake the brûlées for 15–20 minutes, or until a skin forms over the top of each one.

Remove from the oven and from the roasting pan, and refrigerate overnight.

To serve, sprinkle an even amount of the caster sugar on top of each brulee. Quickly place the brûlées under a hot grill (broiler) or gas flame just long enough to caramelise the sugar. Do not allow to scorch.

When the sugar has caramelised, allow the brûlées to cool for 3–4 minutes so that the sugar hardens. Serve immediately with berries and cream.

The baked brûlées will keep in cling film (plastic wrap) for up to 2 days in the refrigerator.

Serves 6–8

Great Moments in Chocolate

1928 Cadbury introduces the famous 'glass and a half' symbol in its advertising campaigns and posters.

Chocolate Delice

Base

90 g (3 oz) unsalted butter

$^1/_3$ cup (90 g, 3 oz) caster (superfine) sugar

2 large eggs

$^3/_4$ cup (90 g, 3 oz) ground almonds

$^1/_4$ cup (30 g, 1 oz) plain (all-purpose) flour, sifted

2 teaspoons cornflour (cornstarch), sifted

Filling

3 teaspoons powdered gelatin

150 mL (5$^1/_2$ fl oz) water

30 mL (1 fl oz) liquid glucose

3 egg yolks

310 g (10 oz) white chocolate, melted

2$^1/_4$ cups (560 mL, 18 fl oz) double (heavy, thickened) cream, whipped

Topping

3 teaspoons powdered gelatin

$^1/_2$ cup (125 mL, 4 fl oz) water

$^1/_4$ cup (60 g, 2 oz) plus 2 tablespoons caster (superfine) sugar

60 g (2 oz) dark chocolate, chopped

2 tablespoons water (extra)

$^1/_4$ cup (30 g, 1 oz) cocoa powder

2 teaspoons cornflour (cornstarch)

Preheat the oven to 180°C (350°F). Line a baking sheet with parchment paper.

To make the base, cream the butter and sugar until light and fluffy. Add the eggs one at a time, beating well after each addition. Fold in the ground almonds, flour and cornflour by hand.

Pour the mixture onto the baking sheet and bake for 5–8 minutes, or until lightly browned. Allow to cool on the tray.

Line the bottom and sides of a clean 23 cm (9 in) springform pan with baking parchment. Cut a 23 cm (9 in) circle out of the base and use to line the bottom of the springform pan.

To make the filling, mix 100 mL (3$^1/_2$ fl oz) of the water and the gelatin together. Dissolve over a hot-water bath. Heat the remaining 50 mL (1$^1/_2$ fl oz) water and the liquid glucose in a saucepan. Blend into the gelatin and allow to cool slightly.

Whisk the egg yolks and the gelatin mixture together. Whisk in the white chocolate and very gently but quickly fold in the whipped cream. Pour over the base and refrigerate for 2 hours or until set.

To make the topping, mix the powdered gelatin and 4 teaspoons of the water together. Dissolve over a hot-water bath. Set aside.

Put the remaining water, the ¼ cup (60 g, 2 oz) caster sugar and dark chocolate in a heavy-based saucepan. Bring to the boil, stirring all the time.

Blend the extra 2 tablespoons water, the 2 tablespoons sugar, cocoa powder and cornflour. Stir into the hot chocolate mixture, stirring all the time. Remove from the heat and mix in the dissolved gelatin. Allow to cool.

When cool, pour the topping slowly over the top of the filling. Chill in the refrigerator for 1 hour before removing from the pan and serving.

This will keep for up to a week in an airtight container in the refrigerator.

Makes 10–12 servings

Chocolate Fudge Cheesecake

375 g (12 oz) chocolate chip cookies
100 g (3½ oz) butter, melted
800 g (26 oz) cream cheese, softened
¼ cup (60 g, 2 oz) caster (superfine) sugar
4 large eggs
250 g (8 oz) dark (plain or semisweet) chocolate, melted
1¼ cups (310 mL, 10 fl oz) double (heavy, thickened) cream, whipped

Preheat the oven to 170°C (325°F). Lightly grease a 23 cm (9 in) springform cake pan and line the bottom with baking parchment.

Crush the chocolate chip cookies in a plastic bag with a rolling pin. Combine with the butter, then spread over the bottom of the prepared pan. Press into the sides and bottom of the pan with the back of a spoon. Set aside.

Beat the cream cheese and caster sugar in a food processor or electric mixer. Add the eggs one at a time, beating well after each addition. Blend in the dark chocolate and finally the whipped cream.

Pour into the prepared base and bake in the oven for 45 minutes.

Turn off the heat and allow the cheesecake to cool in the oven for 2 hours before leaving to chill in the refrigerator.

Carefully remove the cheesecake from the springform pan. Serve in slices with freshly whipped cream or fresh fruits of your choice.

This will keep for up to a week in an airtight container in the refrigerator.

Serves 8–10

Note: To maintain freshness, place a small sheet of wax paper against the side of the cheesecake where a slice has been removed.

What do I do if my chocolate gets too thick?

Chocolate slowly thickens when setting, but can be successfully remelted. If the chocolate has thickened due to overheating, it may be liquefied with the addition of oil or copha (coconut oil), although this will harm the setting properties.

Chocolate Mousse

4 large eggs, separated
150 g (5 oz) dark (plain or semisweet) chocolate
1¼ cups (310 mL, 10 fl oz) double (heavy, thickened)
cream, softly whipped

Whisk the egg whites until stiff peaks form.

Melt the dark chocolate as directed on the packet. Add the egg yolks and stir well.

Quickly but thoroughly stir the chocolate mixture into the cream, then gently but thoroughly fold in the egg whites.

Pour into 1 large or 6–8 small individual serving bowls and chill in the refrigerator until set.

Serve with whipped cream and fresh fruits of your choice.

Can be stored in the refrigerator for 2–3 days. The mousse will drop slightly in volume as the egg whites lose aeration.

Serves 6–8

Great Moments in Chocolate

1936 The 'Energy Ball' bursts onto the market. This vacuum-detonated blob of Horlicks-flavoured dough is later renamed the 'Malteser'. It rapidly becomes the weapon of choice of movie-going children everywhere.

Chocolate Pancakes

2 large eggs

¼ cup (60 g, 2 oz) caster (superfine) sugar

1 cup (250 mL, 8 fl oz) milk

30 g (1 oz) unsalted butter, melted

2 cups (250 g, 8 oz) plain (all-purpose) flour, sifted

1 tablespoon cocoa powder, sifted

1 teaspoon baking powder

maple syrup, to serve

whipped unsalted butter, to serve

icing (confectioners') sugar, for dusting

Whisk the eggs and sugar in a mixing bowl until light and fluffy.

Fold through the milk and melted butter. Fold through the flour, cocoa powder and baking powder, and mix until a smooth batter has formed.

Pour the batter in small amounts (4 tablespoons per pancake) into a lightly oiled frying pan or skillet on a medium heat.

Allow each pancake to cook until the upper surface is full of bubbles. Using a spatula, flip each pancake over as it is ready, to cook on the second side. Each side of the pancake should take no longer than 4 minutes to cook.

Remove the pancakes from the pan and serve immediately with maple syrup, whipped butter and dusted icing sugar.

Serves 4

Chocolate Pashka

¾ cup (125 g, 4 oz) sultanas (golden raisins), chopped
a level ½ cup (100 mL, 3½ fl oz) brandy
125 g (4 oz) butter
⅔ cup (100 g, 3½ oz) icing (confectioners') sugar
½ cup (125 mL, 4 fl oz) sour cream
125 g (4 oz) cream cheese
1 tablespoon lemon juice
grated zest of 1 lemon
1 teaspoon vanilla essence (extract)
½ cup (60 g, 2 oz) chopped toasted almonds
125 g (4 oz) dark (plain or semisweet) chocolate, chopped,
plus extra for decoration
100 g (3½ oz) fresh raspberries, rinsed and hulled
(use canned or frozen raspberries if out of season)
200 g (7 oz) canned mango pulp

Heat the brandy in a small saucepan over a gentle heat until just warm. Remove from the heat and add the sultanas. Let stand until required.

Cream the butter and icing sugar until light and fluffy. Add the sour cream and combine well.

Add the cream cheese, lemon juice and zest, vanilla, almonds, dark chocolate, sultanas and any remaining brandy. Mix well.

Line one large mould 15 cm (6 in) in diameter — or 10 individual moulds — with cheesecloth or fine muslin. Leave enough cloth hanging over the top of the mould to allow for easy removal. Fill the mould with the mixture.

Stand the mould in the refrigerator for 24 hours. Turn onto a serving dish and serve in slices with the raspberries and mango pulp.

Serves 8–10

Chocolate
Peanut Crunch

Base

$1/3$ cup (90 g, 3 oz) unsalted smooth peanut butter

2 tablespoons peanut oil

225 g (7 oz) chocolate-flavoured cookies, crushed

185 g (6 oz) milk chocolate, melted

Topping

1 tablespoon peanut oil

185 g (6 oz) dark (plain or semisweet) chocolate, melted

$1 1/4$ cups (310 mL, 10 fl oz) double (heavy, thickened)
cream, lightly whipped

cocoa powder, for dusting

Line a 28 x 18 cm (11 x 7 in) baking pan with cling film (plastic wrap).

In a large bowl, mix the peanut butter and peanut oil together until a smooth, creamy consistency. Beat in the cookie crumbs and milk chocolate.

Pour the mixture into the prepared pan. Spread evenly and freeze for 30 minutes.

To make the topping, fold the oil into the dark chocolate and then fold in half of the cream. When combined, fold through the remaining cream and ensure all ingredients are combined.

Pour the chocolate mixture on top of the frozen peanut base and return the dessert to the freezer for 6–8 hours. Remove when required.

Using a hot knife, cut the dessert into strips about 3 cm (1 $1/4$ in) wide and 12 cm (4 $1/2$ in) long. Dust with cocoa powder and serve.

Serves 8

Great Moments
in Chocolate

1937 Kit Kat, Rolo and Smarties all hit the shelves for the first time.

Chocolate Peanut Roulade

Buttercream

1/3 cup (90 g, 3 oz) granulated sugar
2/3 cup (150 mL, 5 fl oz) golden syrup *or* corn syrup
1/4 cup plus 1 tablespoon (75 mL, 2 1/2 fl oz) water
3 large egg whites
225 g (7 oz) unsalted butter
2/3 cup (90 g, 3 oz) chopped peanuts

Flourless Sponge

12 level teaspoons instant coffee granules
1/4 cup (60 mL, 2 fl oz) water
6 large eggs, separated
185 g (6 oz) dark (plain or semisweet) chocolate
1/2 cup (125 g, 4 oz) granulated sugar
cocoa powder, for dusting

Ganache

3/4 cup (185 mL, 6 fl oz) single cream
310 g (10 oz) dark (plain or semisweet) chocolate, finely chopped
60 g (2 oz) unsalted butter, softened
finely grated zest of 1 orange
30 mL (1 fl oz) orange liqueur
lightly roasted unsalted peanuts, roughly chopped
icing (confectioners') sugar, for dusting

To make the buttercream, bring the sugar, golden syrup and water to the boil in a heavy-based saucepan. Boil steadily, stirring occasionally, until the syrup registers 118°C (244°F) on a candy thermometer — 2–4 minutes or soft ball stage. Remove from the heat.

When the syrup has cooled to 108°C (224°F), whisk the egg whites in a mixing bowl until stiff peaks form. Continue whisking on a high speed and slowly drizzle in the sugar syrup. Keep whisking until all the syrup is incorporated and the meringue mixture is beginning to cool.

In a separate bowl, whip the butter until it is light and soft, and pale in colour. Add the meringue to the butter in small amounts, whisking as you do so, until thoroughly incorporated.

Finally, add the peanuts and stir through well. Set the buttercream aside until required.

To make the flourless sponge, preheat the oven to 180°C (350°F). Lightly grease a 40 x 35 cm (16 x 14 in) baking pan and line with baking parchment.

Dissolve the instant coffee with the water and blend into the egg yolks. Melt the chocolate over a bowl of hot water. Cool slightly and then mix into the egg yolk mixture.

Using an electric mixer, beat the egg whites until they hold stiff peaks. Continue whisking and, as you do so, gradually incorporate the sugar by sprinkling it slowly down the side of the mixer whilst the machine is still running. Whisk until the sugar has dissolved.

Gently but thoroughly fold in the chocolate mixture and then quickly spread the sponge batter in the prepared baking pan. Bake for 12–15 minutes, or until the cake springs back when touched in the centre.

Place a sheet of greaseproof (wax) paper on top of a clean, damp cloth. Lightly dust the greaseproof paper with cocoa powder. Invert the baked cake onto the paper. Carefully peel away the baking parchment and then quickly roll the sponge from one short edge to the other, making certain that the greaseproof paper rolls in with it.

Allow the rolled sponge to cool on a wire rack until cold, then carefully unroll.

Spread the top of the sponge with the buttercream and then re-roll into a tight cylinder using the damp cloth to assist in getting a firm roll.

Place the rolled sponge in the freezer immediately. Freeze for 1–2 hours before storing covered in the refrigerator until required.

To make the ganache, bring the cream to the boil in a heavy-based saucepan. Add the dark chocolate then remove the pan from the heat. Allow to sit for 2–3 minutes before stirring to a thick, smooth paste.

Allow to cool slightly before whisking through the softened butter and orange zest and liqueur. Refrigerate the ganache until it is of a spreading consistency.

To finish the roulade, spread the sides and top of the rolled sponge with the ganache. Press the peanuts into the ganache and refrigerate for a further 1 hour. Lightly dust with icing sugar before serving.

Serves 12–16

Chocolate Pioneers
Frank Mars
As Henry Ford is to the automobile, Frank Mars is to chocolate. In 1923, Mars launched the Milky Way bar, known outside the United States as the Mars Bar. The widespread success of this product made Frank Mars one of the great democratisers of chocolate.

The superiority of chocolate,
both for health and nourishment,
will soon give it the same preference
over tea and coffee in America
which it has in Spain.

Thomas Jefferson
Letter to John Adams, 1785

Chocolate Pudding with a Melting Middle

225 g (7 oz) unsalted butter, softened
1 level cup (225 g, 7 oz) granulated sugar
225 g (7 oz) dark (plain or semisweet) chocolate, melted
6 large eggs, separated
1½ cups (185 g, 6 oz) plain (all-purpose) flour, sifted
½ teaspoon baking powder (double-acting)
1⅔ cups (185 g, 6 oz) ground almonds
75 g (2½ oz) small dark chocolate squares,
preferably 1 x 1 cm (⅜ x ⅜ in)

Preheat the oven to 180°C (350°F). Lightly brush 8 x 1 cup (250 mL, 8 fl oz) dariole moulds with melted butter and coat the bottom and sides of each mould with sugar.

Cream the butter and sugar until light and fluffy. Add the melted chocolate and mix until combined. Scrape down the sides of the bowl and mix once more to ensure all the chocolate has been thoroughly incorporated.

Add the egg yolks one at a time, beating well after each addition, then add the flour, baking powder and ground almonds. Mix thoroughly.

In a separate bowl, whisk the egg whites until stiff peaks form. Carefully fold into the chocolate mixture.

Place the mixture in an airtight container and refrigerate for 1 hour to set.

Using a small spoon or spatula, coat the inside of each dariole mould with the chilled mixture, approximately 1 cm (⅜ in) thick from the bottom and around the sides, leaving a small hole in the centre of each mould for a square of chocolate.

Insert a square of chocolate into each of the moulds and cover the chocolate and seal the mould with more of the chilled mixture. Place the moulds on a baking sheet and bake in the oven for 30 minutes.

When baked, carefully run a knife around the side of each mould, easing each baked pudding from its container. Unmould each pudding directly onto individual serving plates. Serve immediately with custard or chocolate sauce.

Serves 8

Chocolate Raspberry Luscious

6 large egg yolks

1¼ cups (225 g, 7 oz) icing (confectioners') sugar

250 g (8 oz) unsalted butter, softened

5 tablespoons cocoa powder

150 g (5 oz) dark (plain or semisweet)
chocolate, melted

1¼ cups (310 mL, 10 fl oz) double (heavy, thickened) cream

225 g (7 oz) fresh raspberries

Whisk the egg yolks and half of the icing sugar until thick, light and fluffy. Whip the butter and cocoa powder together until light, fluffy and very soft.

Whisk the dark chocolate into the egg yolk mixture and then add the butter mixture. Combine thoroughly.

Lightly whip cream with the remaining icing sugar. Fold into the chocolate mixture. Just before it is all is folded in, add the raspberries and carefully combine.

Pour the mixture into eight fluted glasses and chill for 1 hour before serving.

Serves 8

Great Moments in Chocolate
1940 As World War II rages around them, the Swiss invent white chocolate.

Chocolate
Self-saucing Pudding

60 g (2 oz) butter
½ cup (125 g, 4 oz) sugar
1 large egg
½ cup (125 mL, 4 fl oz) milk
1 cup (125 g, 4 oz) plain (all-purpose) flour
1 teaspoon baking powder
2 tablespoons cocoa powder
1½ cups (375 mL, 12 fl oz) hot water

Preheat the oven to 180°C (350°F). Grease a 6-cup (1.5 litre, 2½ imp. pint) casserole dish with butter.

Cream the butter and half of the sugar until light and fluffy. Add the egg and beat well.

Sift the flour and baking powder together. Add the milk and sifted flour alternately, mixing until well combined. Pour the batter into the casserole dish.

Mix the cocoa powder and remaining sugar together. Sprinkle over the batter and gently pour the hot water over the top. Bake in the oven for 35–40 minutes.

Serve hot with cream or ice cream.

Serves 4–6

Great Moments
in Chocolate

1941 In response to slow sales during warm weather, Mars produces M&Ms, 'the chocolate that melts in your mouth – not in your hand'.

Chocolate Soufflé

60 g (2 oz) dark (plain or semisweet) chocolate
$^{1}/_{3}$ cup (90 g, 3 oz) sugar
$^{1}/_{2}$ cup (125 g, 4 oz) water
1 large egg
3 egg yolks
5 egg whites
1 $^{1}/_{2}$ tablespoons plain (all-purpose) flour
1 tablespoon cocoa powder
2 tablespoons sugar (extra)

Preheat the oven to 190°C (375°F). Grease a small, 5-cup soufflé dish with butter and then sprinkle sugar over the inside of the dish. Tip away any excess.

Slowly bring the chocolate, one-third of the sugar and water to the boil in a heavy-based saucepan. When the chocolate and sugar have melted, blend the mixture carefully.

Mix 1 egg, the remaining sugar, the flour and cocoa together in a bowl. When smooth and thoroughly combined, add to the hot chocolate mixture. Mix until smooth and return to the heat.

Stir constantly until the mixture thickens — take care not to burn the chocolate or the mixture will become lumpy.

Remove from the heat, add the egg yolks and stir until smooth. Allow to cool.

Whisk the egg whites until soft peaks form. Add the extra 2 tablespoons sugar and beat to a stiff foam. Blend a small amount of the cooled chocolate mixture into the egg whites, and then fold in the remaining chocolate mixture until even in texture.

Spoon into the prepared soufflé dish. Flatten the top of the mixture and run your finger around the inside rim of the dish to ensure that the soufflé rises evenly.

Bake in the oven for 12–15 minutes (about 25–30 minutes for a larger, 6- to 7-cup dish so that the middle will cook). Serve immediately.

Serves 4–5

Chocolate Tart

Pastry

1/2 cup (90 g, 3 oz) icing (confectioners') sugar
2 cups (250 g, 8 oz) plain (all-purpose) flour
4 1/2 tablespoons cocoa powder
185 g (6 oz) unsalted butter
1 large egg

Filling

100 g (3 1/2 oz) butter
100 g (3 1/2 oz) dark (plain or semisweet) chocolate
3 large eggs
1/3 cup (45 g, 1 1/2 oz) plain (all-purpose) flour, sifted
2/3 cup (150 g, 5 oz) caster (superfine) sugar

Topping

a level 1/2 cup (100 mL, 3 1/2 fl oz) double (heavy, thickened) cream
250 g (8 oz) dark (plain or semisweet) chocolate, chopped

Preheat the oven to 150°C (300°F). Lightly grease a 24 x 4 cm (10 x 1 3/4 in) quiche or round cake pan.

To make the pastry, sift the icing sugar, flour and cocoa powder into a bowl. Rub the butter into the dry ingredients until the mixture resembles fine breadcrumbs. Add the egg and work the mixture to a dough.

On a lightly floured surface, roll the dough thinly and large enough in size to fill the greased pan. Line the pan carefully with the pastry and place in the refrigerator until the filling is ready.

To make the filling, melt the butter and chocolate together in the top of a double boiler.

Whisk the eggs, flour and sugar on a high speed for 5 minutes. Pour in the chocolate mixture and mix until combined.

Pour the filling into the pastry-lined pan and bake in the oven for 35–45 minutes.

Make the topping while the tart is baking. Bring the cream slowly to the boil in a heavy-based saucepan. Remove from the heat and add the dark chocolate, stirring until all the chocolate has dissolved. Let the mixture stand in the saucepan, covered, until the tart has baked and cooled.

When the tart is baked, allow to cool in the pan. As it cools, the filling will sink — help it to flatten by pressing it down gently.

When the tart is cold and the filling flattened, pour the chocolate topping over the top. Refrigerate for 1 hour before serving.

Serves 8–10

Chocolate Terrine with Nut Crust

½ cup (45 g, 1½ oz) walnuts
½ cup (45 g, 1½ oz) hazelnuts
3 egg yolks
½ cup (125 g, 4 oz) caster (superfine) sugar
150 g (5 oz) unsalted butter, softened
¾ cup (90 g, 3 oz) cocoa powder
75 g (2½ oz) dark (plain or semisweet) chocolate
1 cup (250 mL, 8 fl oz) double (heavy, thickened) cream
2½ tablespoons icing (confectioners') sugar
fresh fruit, to garnish
fresh mint, to garnish

Roast the walnuts and hazelnuts in the oven until light golden brown. Remove the husks from the hazelnuts by rolling together in a kitchen cloth, then grind all the nuts to medium-fine.

Brush a 21 x 7.5 cm (8 x 3 in) loaf pan or mould with melted butter, coating well. Place the ground nuts in the mould, then roll around until all sides are evenly coated. Tip out and reserve any excess nuts, then place the pan in the refrigerator to firm the nut coating.

Whisk the egg yolks and caster sugar together until pale. In a separate bowl, cream the butter and cocoa powder with a wooden spoon.

Melt the dark chocolate over a pot of simmering water. Add to the egg yolk mixture, whisking continuously as you do so until well combined. Now combine with the butter mixture.

Semi-whip the cream and icing sugar, then add to the chocolate mixture. Stir until smooth.

Using a piping bag, half-fill the pan with the chocolate mixture, making sure there are no air pockets. Fill with the remaining chocolate and tap the edges of the pan lightly to remove any air. Sprinkle the reserved nuts over the top and place the pan in the refrigerator for about 3 hours to allow the terrine to set.

To serve, quickly dip the pan in hot water, then turn the terrine out onto a cutting board. Using a warm knife, cut the terrine into even slices. Garnish with the fresh fruit and mint, and serve with a berry coulis and a little whole fruit.

Serves 8

Creamy Chocolate Mousse

125 g (4 oz) cream cheese
150 g (5 oz) caster (superfine) sugar
2 large egg yolks
2½ cups (625 mL, 1 imp. pint) double (heavy, thickened) cream
125 g (4 oz) dark (plain or semisweet) chocolate, melted
120 g (4 oz) milk chocolate, melted

Beat the cream cheese, sugar and egg yolks until smooth. (The sugar may not dissolve completely.)

Whip the cream until stiff and return to the refrigerator until required.

Quickly stir the dark and milk chocolates into the smooth cream cheese mixture and immediately fold through the whipped cream by hand. (The warmth of your hand will help the stiff chocolate to fold through the cream. Any remaining sugar granules will dissolve during setting.)

Spoon the mousse into six glasses and chill for 30 minutes before serving.

Serves 6

Chocolate Fondue

selection of fresh fruits (such as strawberries, grapes, pineapple chunks or mandarin or orange segments) for dipping

¼ cup (60 mL, 2 fl oz) Grand Marnier *or* your favourite liqueur

⅔ cup (150 mL, 5 fl oz) liquid glucose *or* corn sugar

⅔ cup (150 mL, 5 fl oz) double (heavy, thickened) cream

250 g (8 oz) dark (plain or semisweet) chocolate, chopped

Place the fresh fruits and half of the Grand Marnier in a bowl. Allow to macerate for 1 hour.

Gently bring the liquid glucose, cream and remaining Grand Marnier to the boil in a saucepan, stirring all the time.

Remove the pan from the heat, add the chocolate and stir until all the ingredients are combined.

If you don't have a fondue set, consisting of a large bowl set above a small flame, serve the fondue in a warmed bowl and set it in the centre of the selection of macerated fruits for dipping.

Serves 6–8

Note: You can substitute the dark (plain or semisweet) chocolate with white or milk chocolate in this recipe. You can also make one mixture from all three types of chocolate by pouring them into one dish just before serving and allowing them to become a marbled mass.

If a recipe asks for couverture but it is unavailable or too expensive, can I use another chocolate?

Couverture is a French term describing a type or style, and refers to the quality and richness in cocoa butter. If couverture is unavailable, use any high-quality substitute.

Marbled Chocolate Pie

225 g (7 oz) plain sweet cookies

1 teaspoon ground cinnamon

125 g (4 oz) butter, melted

2 large eggs, separated

3 teaspoons powdered gelatin

a level $\frac{1}{3}$ cup (75 g, $2\frac{1}{2}$ oz) caster (superfine) sugar

1 cup (250 mL, 8 fl oz) milk

$\frac{1}{4}$ cup (60 mL, 2 fl oz) dark rum

375 g (12 oz) dark (plain or semisweet) chocolate, chopped

2 tablespoons icing (confectioners') sugar

1 teaspoon vanilla essence (extract)

1 cup (250 mL, 8 fl oz) double (heavy, thickened) cream, whipped

Preheat the oven to 160°C (325°F). Grease and flour a 23 cm (9 in) springform cake pan.

Process or crush the cookies into fine crumbs. Mix thoroughly with the cinnamon and butter. Spread over the bottom of the prepared pan and press into the sides and bottom with the back of a spoon. Bake in the oven for 15 minutes. Allow to cool.

Lightly beat the egg yolks. Using a double boiler, gently heat the egg yolks, gelatine, $\frac{1}{4}$ cup (60 g, 2 oz) of the caster sugar, milk, rum and dark chocolate. Stir until the chocolate has melted and the mixture thickens. Remove from the heat and set aside until cold.

Whisk the egg whites until stiff peaks form. Whisk in the remaining caster sugar until meringue forms. Fold into the chocolate mixture.

Fold the icing sugar and vanilla essence into the cream. Place alternate spoonfuls of the chocolate and cream mixtures into the crumb crust.

When all the mixtures have been poured into the crumb crust, drag a small knife through the chocolate and cream mixtures, being careful not to touch the crumb crust, to achieve a marbling effect. Place in the refrigerator for about 3 hours to set.

When set, remove the pan and transfer to a serving plate.

If not serving immediately, cover with cling film (plastic wrap) and keep in the refrigerator until ready to use.

Serves 8–10

White Chocolate Marquise

2 teaspoons powdered gelatin

1 1/2 tablespoons water

1 1/2 tablespoons liquid glucose

3 large egg yolks

250 g (8 oz) white chocolate, melted

1 2/3 cups (400 mL, 13 fl oz) double (heavy, thickened) cream, softly whipped

24 savoiardi biscuits (sponge fingers)

fresh orange segments, pips removed, to serve

Soak the powdered gelatin in the water. Place the soaked gelatin and liquid glucose in a saucepan and gently heat until melted. Remove and allow to cool for 30 seconds.

Whisk the egg yolks into the gelatin mixture, then add the white chocolate. Stir with a wooden spoon until smooth.

Pour the white chocolate mixture into the cream, stirring quickly to blend. This makes the chocolate marquise.

Stand the savoiardi biscuits upright around the side of a 20 cm (8 in) springform cake pan. Cover the bottom of the pan with any remaining biscuits.

Pour the chocolate marquise into the pan, tapping gently to ensure it flows into any holes. Refrigerate for 1 hour to allow the marquise to set before serving wedges with fresh orange segments.

Serves 12

Great Moments in Chocolate

1982 The world's annual consumption of chocolate passes 600 000 tonnes.

White Chocolate Rose Petal Mousse

2 teaspoons powdered gelatin

1½ tablespoons water

45 mL (1½ fl oz) liquid glucose

2 large egg yolks

250 g (8 oz) white chocolate buttons, melted

2½ cups (625 mL, 1 imp. pint) double (heavy, thickened) cream,
very lightly whipped

juice and zest of 1 lemon

petals of 3 medium-size roses in different hues, rinsed and dried*

Raspberry Sauce

225 g (7 oz) fresh raspberries, hulled and rinsed

2½ tablespoons cold water

sugar, to sweeten

Soak the powdered gelatin in the water. Place the soaked gelatin and liquid glucose in a saucepan and gently heat until melted.

Whisk in the egg yolks, then stir in the white chocolate.

Pour the white chocolate mixture into the cream, stirring quickly to blend, then add the lemon juice and zest and rose petals. Stir through gently.

Pour mixture into a 30 x 25 x 3 cm (12 x 10 x 1½ in) baking pan lined with cling film (plastic wrap). Refrigerate for about 1½ hours until firm.

To make the raspberry sauce, place the raspberries and water into a blender with enough sugar to sweeten. Purée until smooth.

When the mousse is set, cut into 5 cm (2 in) squares and serve on the raspberry sauce. Allow 2 squares per serving.

Serves 8–10

*Rose petals should be separated from stems and stamens, and washed carefully before use.

Great Moments in Chocolate

1982 NASA issues its space shuttle astronauts with rations that include M&Ms.

chocolate providores of the world

The following is a list that includes some of the better known chocolate companies, some smaller companies that manufacture chocolate from bean to bar, and a sprinkling of shops and stores that add their own remarkable signature to manufactured chocolate by remoulding and flavouring it on the premises.

Ackermans
9 Goldhurst Terrace
Finchley Road
London NW6 3HX
United Kingdom
tel (44 171) 482 3731
fax (44 171) 482 4651
Begun in the 1940s as a family business with a weekly output of 50 kg (100 lb), Ackermans is today one of Britain's major handmade chocolate specialists, producing 3000 kg (6000 lb) of chocolate per week — a growth that was boosted in 1969 when the Queen Mother awarded the company a royal warrant. On the death in the early 1990s of the founder Werner Ackerman, the company passed into the hands of a team of owner–directors: Franz Hippel (Master Chocolatier and Managing Director), Anthony Charlton (Sales Director) and Valerie Miller (Packaging Director). Heavy investment in the latest technology and expanded production facilities have enabled Ackermans to maintain a global pace, focusing on an export drive to Europe and the United States, while maintaining its traditional mail order service.

Baker's Chocolate
General Foods Consumer Centre
250 North Street
White Plains
NY 10625
United States of America
Written enquiries only

Founded in 1765 in Dorchester, Massachusetts, by a local physician Dr James Baker and the Irish immigrant and chocolate maker John Hannon, Baker's was the first chocolate mill in the America colonies. The business proceeded as a partnership until 1779 when Hannon was lost at sea on a cocoa-buying expedition and the company fell into the sole ownership of Baker. In 1824, the doctor's grandson bestowed his own name on the company — Walter Baker — under which it operated as a family enterprise for more than 100 years. In 1927, the company became part of what is today Kraft Foods.

In addition to being one of the oldest American companies, Baker's also owns one of America's oldest trademarks, 'La Belle Chocolatiere' (the beautiful chocolate seller), which is based on a 1745 painting by Swiss artist Jean Etienne Liotard. The painting is a portrait of Anna Baltauf, who was a young waitress in a Vienna chocolate house when she met an Austrian aristocrat, Prince Dietrichstein. The couple married and the Prince commissioned the painting, in which Anna appears as he first saw her, in her chocolate server's costume. More than a century later, a Walter Baker executive noticed the portrait in the Dresden Art Gallery in Germany; in 1872, the image became part of Baker's advertising and is still used today on Baker's packaging and chocolates.

Baratti & Milano
Via Nannetti 1
40069 Zola Predosa (Bologna)
Italy
tel (39 51) 617 2777
fax (39 51) 617 2769

A company founded in 1858 by Ferdinando Baratti and Eduardo Milano. In 1875, the Mayor of Bologna presented Baratti and Milano with the royal family's coat of arms, which the company has used as an emblem ever since.

Barry Callebaut International
Aalsterstraat 122
B–9280
Lebbeke-Wieze
Belgium
tel (32 53) 730 211
fax (32 53) 730 420

Callebaut began in the 1850s as a family-run malt plant, brewery and dairy. In 1890, the company diversified into confectionery production and in 1911 began to build a reputation for high-quality couvertures. By 1965, Callebaut had established a worldwide network, leading to expanded sales in the 1970s. The company established training colleges in Belgium and Singapore. In the 1980s, the family sold the business to the C.J. Van Houten and Zoon AG company, although the Callebaut family's involvement in chocolate making has continued in Canada, where Bernard Callebaut went on to found the Bernard Callebaut Chocolate Company.

In 1997, Callebaut International merged with Cacao Barry, forming Barry Callebaut. The company produces and sells chocolate around the world.

Bendicks of Mayfair
46 Curzon Street
London W1Y 7RF
United Kingdom
tel (44 1962) 844 800
fax (44 1962) 841 547

A company founded in the late 1920s, whose name is a conflation of the surnames of its owners Benson and Dickson. Bendicks began in Kensington, London, and later acquired a factory in Perivale to meet an ever increasing demand from its London shops, particularly in Mayfair.

In 1955, Bendicks amalgamated with Cox's 'Royal Winchester Chocolates', which, like Bendicks, had earlier suspended its production of pastries in order to focus on its chocolate making side. The new company became Bendicks (Mayfair) Limited, and concentrated all its production facilities at Winchester. It received a royal warrant in 1962.

Bernachon
42 Cours Franklin Roosevelt
69006 Lyon
France
tel (33 78) 24 3798
fax (33 78) 52 6977

Of course, any trip to France would not be complete without trying to visit as many chocolate companies as you possibly can. If you are in the vicinity of Lyon, a slight detour to Bernachon is an absolute must. The founders and owners, Jean-Jacques and Maurice Bernachon, can be found on site creating their delicacies. As with many of the world's chocolate stores, the feature item in the store would have to be the Palet D'or — they're so fresh and it would be a sin not to try them.

Blommer Chocolate Company
PO Box 45
East Greenville
PA 18041
United States of America
tel (1 215) 679 4472
fax (1 215) 679 4196

This company was founded in Chicago in 1939 by three brothers — Henry, Al and Bernard Blommer. The company now has three plants strategically located across the USA: in Chicago; near San Francisco; and in East Greenville, Pennsylvania. Each of these plants maintains strict quality controls — from the standard of the cocoa beans they import to the finished products that are shipped to their customers around the world. Blommer Chocolate Company manufactures a full line of chocolate products including chocolate and compound coating, chocolate chips, and a wide colour and flavour spectrum of Dutch processed cocoas for the dairy, baking and confectionery industries.

Bonbon Jeanette
Europaplain 87
1078 GZ Amsterdam
The Netherlands
tel (31 20) 664 9638
fax (31 20) 675 6543

See 'My Favourite Chocolatiers', page 173.

Brown and Haley
PO Box 1596
Tacoma
Washington 98401
United States of America
tel (1 206) 593 3000
fax (1 206) 272 6742

Founded in Washington State, USA, Brown and Haley are renowned for just one bar, although they produce a wide range of chocolate products. Launched in 1923, the Almond Roca bar has been consistently popular throughout the United States. Since J.C. Haley, a sales and advertising man, and Harry L. Brown, a confectioner, teamed up in 1906, they had marketed a range of chocolates and confections. Their crunchy, log-shaped Mountain Bar was renamed Almond Roca by a local librarian and from that point on, they never looked back.

Cadbury Schweppes Pty Ltd
323 Canterbury Road
Ringwood
Victoria 3134
Australia
tel (61 3) 9210 1530
fax (61 3) 9879 7121

When Cadbury and Fry decided to build a confectionery factory in Australia, they were joined in the venture by the Pascall firm (Pascall Murray Company). Claremont, near Hobart, was chosen as the location for the new factory. The nearby Derwent River provided access for ships and the region offered a consistent supply of fresh milk. Production began in 1922 with the manufacture of Pascall products. Six years later, Claremont began to produce the now famous Cadbury Dairy Milk chocolate and Cadbury Bournville Cocoa.

The company continued to grow in the Australian region, merging with a New Zealand baking company, Hudson & Co., in 1930.

After the acquisition of MacRobertson Chocolates in 1967, Ringwood, outside Melbourne, became the site of Cadbury's second Australian factory. In Britain, Cadbury merged with Schweppes in 1969, and in 1970 the Australian branches of the company followed suit. Expansion continued in 1984 when Cadbury established a cocoa grinding facility in Jurong, Singapore. Operating as MacRobertson Foods Pty Ltd, this plant processes cocoa beans into cocoa mass, cocoa butter and powder for use by Cadbury manufacturing plants in the Asia–Pacific region.

In 1986, Cadbury Australia purchased the Cadbury New Zealand operations from its parent company, Cadbury Schweppes PLC, and the following year the company purchased Red Tulip Chocolates, a US firm. Red Tulip is now the number one selling Easter egg brand in Australia. Further acquisitions followed and in 1994 construction commenced on a new Cadbury manufacturing plant in Beijing, China. Completed in 1995, this plant produces a range of Cadbury chocolate products as well as Cadbury chocolate eclairs and drinking chocolate. In Australia, the Claremont and Ringwood sites now manufacture a major proportion of Australian chocolate and sugar confectionery. Cadbury's well-known brands are in many cases market leaders; they include Cadbury, Red Tulip, Pascall, Fry, Trebor, MacRobertson, Unicorp and Europe.

Cadbury Chocolates Limited
Bournville
Birmingham B3O 2LU
United Kingdom
tel (44 21) 451 4180
John Cadbury first started selling tea and coffee in Birmingham in 1824, and by 1831 he was also manufacturing and selling drinking chocolates and cocoas. The business grew and prospered, and under the guidance of John's sons, Richard and George, moved into new, modern premises in Bournville in 1879. This is still the site of one of the company's factories, and the Bournville name is an important Cadbury brand.

Early chocolate confectionery was very coarse and dry. George Cadbury Junior, grandson of the founder, met the challenge presented by manufacturing improvements on the continent by investing in research and a new plant, and in 1905 Cadbury Dairy Milk chocolate was born. In 1919, Cadbury Brothers merged with J.S. Fry & Sons of Bristol, whose product range complemented Cadbury's. Many of the Fry brands, such as Fry's Turkish Delight, are still popular today.

World War I brought advances in machinery and technology which benefited the chocolate industry when peace returned. More efficient machinery, plentiful raw ingredients and lower transport costs transformed chocolate from a luxury into a product that was more and more affordable for most people. The inter-war years saw constant rebuilding at the Bournville factory, a process that resumed in 1960.

As the company grew, it acquired new factory sites: a milk processing plant in Marlbrook, a large factory at Moreton, and a specialist cocoa bean processing plant at Chirk in North Wales, which today operates for 24 hours a day, 7 days a week, processing the 50 000 tonnes of cocoa beans per year. In 1995, Cadbury Schweppes bought the US giant Dr Pepper, as well as the Canadian chocolate manufacturer Nielson. Today, Cadbury Schweppes manufactures its products in more than 60 countries and trades in more than 120.

Caffarel
Via Gianavello 41
10062 Luserna S. Giovanni
Torino
Italy
tel (39 11) 900 344
fax (39 11) 901 853

The Caffarel factory was opened outside Turin in the early 1800s. An adjacent river turned a hydraulic wheel that powered the cocoa mill. In 1852, Caffarel invented *gianduiotti*, a new variety of chocolate, by blending cocoa powder and sugar.

Chocolats Camille Bloch
CH–2608 Courtelary
Switzerland
tel (41 39) 44 17 17
fax (41 39) 44 10 38

In the year of the Wall Street Crash, 1929, Camille Bloch began making chocolates from his home in Bern, Switzerland, using industrially manufactured chocolate. In 1933, he moved to Belpstrasse and began manufacturing chocolate from cocoa beans, entering a market dominated by the descendants of the founding fathers of the Swiss chocolate industry. With the Depression still stinging, Bloch moved into an old paper pulp factory in Courtelary in 1935.

As the Depression passed, the business expanded, but in 1939 the outbreak of World War II in Europe led to shortages of raw products and an end to the supply of cocoa beans. The ever-resourceful Bloch began mixing small quantities of chocolate with hazelnuts, which were still available from Turkey and Spain, producing 'Ragusa' and, in 1948, 'Torino'.

Innovation continued to characterise the company. After the death of its founder in 1970, at the age of 80, expansion continued under the direction of his son, Rolf. In 1980, for example, Chocolats Camille Bloch opened a laboratory for the control and analysis of raw materials. Today the company employs 200 people and produces 12–15 tonnes of chocolate daily. Camille Bloch ranks fourth amongst Switzerland's brand-name chocolates, and has annual sales worth 40 million Swiss francs.

Charbonnel et Walker
1 The Royal Arcade
28 Old Bond Street
London W1X 4BT
United Kingdom
tel (44 171) 491 0939

It was Edward VII, then Prince of Wales, who in 1875 encouraged Madame Charbonnel to leave her Paris chocolate house, Maison Boissier, to join a Mrs Walker in establishing a fine confectionery house in London. More than a century later, in 1989, the company returned to private ownership and introduced an innovative selection of chocolate truffle sauces, molinillos, jugs and drinking chocolate.

Chocolaterie Bernard Callebaut
1313 1st Street SE
Calgary
Alberta T2G 5L1
Canada
tel (1 403) 265 5777
fax (1 403) 265 7738

Bernard Callebaut is the fourth generation of the famous Belgian chocolate manufacturing family. In the late 1970s, when his father and uncle died, the company was sold to the Suchard Toblerone group, but Bernard Callebaut maintained the family tradition by working for a chocolate factory in Antwerp. In 1983 Callebaut emigrated to Canada and set up shop in Calgary.

Chocolaterie Guylian N.V.
Europark-OOST–1
9100 Saint Niklaas
Belgium
tel (32 3) 778 07 77
fax (32 3) 777 06 81

Founded by Guy and Liliane Foubert, Guylian's chocolates are sold in 72 countries, and the new production facilities in Saint Niklaas produce more than 75 tonnes of chocolate per day. Guylian is perhaps most noted for its marbled chocolate seashells with fine praline filling.

Chocolatier
244 Waterdale Road
Ivanhoe
Victoria 3079
Australia
tel (61 3) 9499 7022
fax (61 3) 9499 6438
Begun as a small business in 1986 and incorporated in 1988,
Chocolatier is run by the Grisold family, especially David, John and
Mark Grisold, the public faces of the company. Chocolatier supplies
most major Australian hotels, airlines, resorts, hospitals and caterers,
as well as the entertainment industry. Chocolatier has also spent much
time and effort producing a range of long-life chocolate fillings for use
in their new retail range, ensuring that quality and freshness of taste
and flavour are not diminished.

Because of its high reputation, major manufacturers often request the
company to evaluate new lines or product changes. With its fine
tradition of Belgian-style chocolate and the freshest of raw ingredients,
the future of Chocolatier in the Australian and international
marketplace is assured.

Côte de France
9 Avenue Du President Salvador-Allende
94400 Vitry-Sur-Seine
France
tel (33 1) 4680 8506
fax (33 1) 4681 9263
Founded in 1936, Côte de France is one of very few Parisian
manufacturers that still produces chocolate entirely on site —
beginning with beans especially selected to give the final product a
long, delicate finish.

Côte D'or
Rue Barastraat 40
B–1070 Bruxelles
Belgium
Written enquiries only
The symbol of this company, an elephant with its trunk raised, has
remained unchanged for more than a century. Founded in 1870 by
the father of the invention of pralines, Charles Neuhaus, Côte D'or
has been a benchmark for the production of quality chocolates. Once

made from the cocoa beans that arrived at the Antwerp docks, Côte D'or's chocolate can today be found in a variety of department stores around the globe.

Dilettante Chocolates
416 Broadway
Seattle WA 98122
United States of America
tel (1 206) 328 1530
Situated in the heart of the Seattle restaurant and nightlife area of Broadway, Dilettante is a venue in itself: chocolate store, cake and pastry bakery, and a coffee shop/restaurant. In addition, the story of Dilettante is a romantic tale which is typical of the history of chocolate.

The story begins with Julius Rudolph Franzen, a Budapest-born, French- and Viennese-trained pastry chef who, in a private notebook, recorded a series of 'master formulas' which he developed in the service of two monarchs: the Emperor Franz Josef of Austria and Czar Nicholas II of Russia. Julius moved to the United States prior to World War I, escaping the Russian Revolution. He later taught the secret formulas to his brother-in-law, Earl Remington Davenport, who in turn passed them on to his children. With the aid of the master formulas, the Earl's grandson, Dana Taylor Davenport, is now the force behind Dilettante Chocolates. A catalogue of the company's extensive range is available for mail orders.

Dreimeister
Weststrasse 47–49
D–59457 Werl
Westonnen
Germany
tel (49 29) 22 820 45
fax (49 29) 22 852 52
Started in 1953 by the father of the present *maître chocolatier*, Hans Wilhelm Schroder, Dreimeister was initially known as Cafe Schroder. Its original location was in the shadow of the Basilica in the pilgrim town of Werl. The name Dreimeister was adopted in 1973, and a large production unit was opened in 1988 in a converted dairy.

Droste B.V.
PO Box 5
8170 AA Vaasen
The Netherlands
Written enquiries only

Droste began production of chocolate in 1890, and in 1898 obtained the right to display the royal coat of arms of the Netherlands. In addition to an international reputation for premium quality chocolate, Droste is famous for its 'Droste nurse' logo, which first appeared on packaging in 1909 and remains unchanged to this day.

Ferrero Canada Ltd.
Suite 900, 100 Sheppard Ave E.
North York
Ontario M2N 6N5
Canada
tel (1 416) 590 0775
fax (1 416) 590 0709
Loved by adults for the Ferrero Rocher and by children for Kinder Surprise and Nutella, Ferrero is a giant of the world confectionery industry. Ferrero also produces the Mon Cheri brand and all products can be found in chocolate stores and supermarkets worldwide.

Fran's Chocolates
2805 East Madison
Seattle
Washington 98122–4020
United States of America
tel (1 206) 322 0233
I was at the end of my stay in Seattle when I first heard about Fran's. The store is a treat for the eyes and soul for the chocolate lover. It stocks a small selection of exquisite pastries and cakes, along with Fran's renowned chocolates, chocolate bars and sauces. In addition to the products, a black and gold decor and polished wooden floors make this an oasis. Fran's also has a mail order service.

Ghirardelli Chocolate Co.
PO Box 5098
San Leandro
CA 94577–0550
United States of America
tel (1800) 877 9338
or
900 North Point St
San Francisco, CA
United States of America
tel (1 415) 474 1414

The Ghirardelli Chocolate Co. was founded by Domingo Ghirardelli, who was born in 1817 in Rapallo, Italy. As a youth, he served as a confectioner's apprentice in Genoa, then at age 20, he married and emigrated with his wife to South America. After working in a coffee company in Uruguay, Ghirardelli moved to Lima, Peru, where he opened his first business, and where his young wife tragically died. In 1848, a friend, James Lick, moved to California, taking with him 600 pounds of Ghirardelli's chocolate, which he sold very quickly and easily. James Lick advised Ghirardelli to come to California where there were many great opportunities for a young chocolate maker. Ghirardelli did so the following year.

After initially joining the Californian gold rush, Ghirardelli opened a store in San Francisco selling supplies to miners. He brought his new family from Peru and, in 1850, opened a confectionery store named French Soda Fountain. One of San Francisco's great fires destroyed his businesses, but by 1853 he was importing more than 200 pounds of cocoa a year. After passing the company to his sons in 1885, the renamed Pioneer Eagle Chocolate Manufactory focused it efforts on chocolate, coffee and spices, a strategy that paid off. By 1889, the business was employing 30 workers and selling more than 50 000 pounds of chocolate annually. The company, named Ghirardelli Chocolate, is still trading today.

Godiva Chocolatier
260 Madison Ave
New York
NY 10016
United States of America
tel (1 212) 951 2888

247 Regent Street
London, W1
United Kingdom
tel (44 171) 495 2845

Godiva Cafe
Level 2, Unit 35
Hilton International Hotel
Singapore
tel (65) 735 3986
See 'My Favourite Chocolatiers', page 176.

Guittard Chocolate Co.
10 Guittard Road
Burlingame
San Francisco CA
United States of America
Written enquiries only
In 1868, Etienne Guittard, a former employee in his uncle's chocolate factory in Paris and a failed prospector in the Californian gold rush, established Guittard Chocolate in San Francisco. Guittard prospered, survived the great San Francisco earthquake of 1906, and eventually built a factory in Burlingame, near the San Francisco airport.

Haigh's Chocolates
153 Greenhill Road
Parkside
South Australia 5063
Australia
tel (61 8) 271 3294
fax (61 8) 373 0528
Alf Haigh opened the first Haigh's chocolate shop in 1915, in Adelaide, South Australia, founding Australia's longest lasting family-owned chocolate company. Alf's son Claude joined Haigh's in 1921 and spent some time working at Lindt and Sprungli in Switzerland. Alf's descendants still run the company today. At their Parkside factory, it is now possible for visitors to view the entire chocolate-making process.

Hershey Chocolate USA
Hershey
PA 17033–0815
United States of America
tel (1 717) 534 4200
Despite his immense wealth at the time of his death, Milton Hershey, the founder of Hershey Chocolate, began small. In the early 1900s, at the age of 43, Hershey sold a minor caramel confectionery company and bought the site in Pennsylvania where the Hershey factory and the Hershey model town both stand today. The Hershey Kiss, released in 1907, was the first of the company's many successes. Hershey used some of his riches to build the town of Hershey for his employees, complete with a school, church and other institutions. He also founded an orphanage and school for orphan boys.

House of Brussels Chocolates
208–750 Terminal Street
Vancouver
British Columbia
Canada
Written enquiries only

House of Brussels is one of a number of chocolate companies that has factories in and around British Columbia, Canada. The company has a large factory just a little from the centre of town and is renowned for its quality range of chocolate products featuring distinctive, sophisticated packaging and upmarket stores around the province.

Joseph Terry and Sons Ltd
Bishopthorpe Road
York YO1 1YE
United Kingdom
Written enquiries only

This company is famed worldwide for virtually a single product: the chocolate orange, a ball of milk chocolate flavoured with orange oil and wrapped in orange foil. Joseph Terry and Sons was founded in York, England, in 1767 and today produces its orange chocolate in the traditional 'orange' shape, as well as in bars and blocks, for sale around the world. Terrys is also famed for its 'Twilights' box of chocolates featuring dark-chocolate-enrobed individual pieces.

La Maison du Chocolat
225 Rue du Fauborg-St-Honoré
Paris 75008
France
tel (33 1) 4227 3944

Robert Linxe, master chocolatier, creates chocolates that are well worth the trip to France to enjoy, even though his products can be found in other countries these days. Robert is famed for the mouth-watering centres, truffle fillings and flavours that he creates daily — ginger, mint, citrus and herb fillings are amongst the plethora of flavours to choose from when enjoying chocolates from this aromatic store.

Laura Secord Inc
Box/C.P. 7200
Willowdale B,
Ontario M2K 2Z2
Canada

tel (1800) 268 6353
fax (1 416) 218 2762
Unlike most chocolate companies, Laura Secord Inc. is not named after
its founder, but after a Canadian heroine (see page 51). The company is
based in Toronto, Canada, and has numerous store-fronts featuring
quality packaged and individual chocolates made at its factory. In 1986,
the company joined the global giant Nestlé.

Le Chocolaterie Bruyerre
Chausee de Bruxelles 47
B 6401 Gosselies
Belgium
tel (32 71) 85 22 42
fax (32 71) 85 33 38
Founded in 1909, this small chocolate firm has won the hearts and
taste buds of many who have visited its Belgium home. It is famed for
the intensity of the flavours that fill the Belgian chocolate shells of
truffles and dipped chocolates.

Leonidas
Royal Hiberian Way
Dublin 2
Ireland
(353 1) 679 5915
Greek American Leonidas Kesdekidis founded Leonidas chocolates
after visiting the Belgian World Fair in 1910. In 1911, he began what is
today a company in command of more than 1500 stores throughout
Europe and North America.

Lindt & Sprungli
Seestrasse 204
CH — 8802 Kilchberg
Switzerland
tel (41 1) 716 22 33
fax (41 1) 715 39 85
It was Rodolphe Lindt, a chocolate manufacturer in Bern,
Switzerland, who in 1879 developed conching, opening the way for
the world's first melting or fondant chocolate. Lindt died in 1909, at
which time his business was bought by members of the Sprungli
family — who were famous chocolate makers in their own right —
for 1.5 million Swiss francs. Two of the greatest names in chocolate
were thus united to form Lindt & Sprungli.

M&M/Mars
A Division of Mars Inc
High Street
Hackettstown
NJ 07840
United States of America
tel (1 201) 852 1000
Founded by Franklin (Frank) Mars, the company is now the largest family-owned confectionery company in the world. In 1911, Frank Mars began making candy from his home in Tacoma, Washington, but within a decade he had moved to a factory in Minneapolis, Minnesota. In 1923, Mars introduced the Mars Milky Way bar, an enormous success. In 1940, his son Forrest E. Mars Snr returned to the USA after almost a decade building confectionery and other businesses in Britain. He quickly set about establishing M&M Limited in Newark, New Jersey, a company that in 1967 joined the Mars confectionery businesses under the consolidated banner of M&M/Mars.

Nestlé Canada Inc
Box/C.P 7200
Willowdale B.
Ontario M2K 2Z2
Canada
tel (416) 218 2681
fax (416) 218 2762
One of the numerous divisions of the world's largest food company, Nestlé Canada owns the Laura Secord Chocolate Company. Nestlé was founded by Henri Nestlé, who developed condensed milk and child's formulas. In 1875, Daniel Peter used Nestlé's condensed milk to make milk chocolate. Nestlé and Peter joined forces and eventually the Nestlé company purchased some of the world's best chocolate companies and manufacturers (along with other food companies), such as Cailler and Willy Wonka Chocolate Co., to become the world's most powerful food and chocolate company.

Neuhaus USA
97–45 Queens Boulevard
Suite 503, Rego Park
New York 11374
United States of America
tel (212) 897 6000

In 1857, Jean Neuhaus left his native Switzerland to settle in Brussels, Belgium. With his brother-in-law, a pharmacist, he opened a pharmacy and confectionery store, selling cough drops, liquorice (for heartburn) and bars of dark chocolate. When Jean's son Fredrick became an apprentice, he showed far more interest in the confections than the pharmaceuticals, and in 1912 Fredrick's son Jean began to build the business into a large chocolate company. Neuhaus, which is no longer in the hands of the family, has numerous stores around the world.

Ortrud Munch Carstens
425 East 58th Street
New York
NY 10022
United States of America
tel (1 212) 751 9591
This creative whizz produces chocolates for sale in numerous locations around New York city (including the popular Dean and Deluca coffee stores) and outside of Manhattan. She is renowned for her 'rusty tools' — chocolates moulded into the shape of tools and dusted with cocoa powder. She is equally famed for the high quality of the ingredients she uses.

Prestat
14 Princess Arcade
Piccadilly
London SW1Y 6DS
United Kingdom
tel (44 171) 629 4838
Prestat began trading in 1902, in London's Oxford Street, making it one of the oldest chocolate houses in England. In 1974, the Queen awarded the company a royal warrant, and Prestat still supplies Buckingham Palace with a range of chocolate delights. The company is particularly famed for its truffles, which are produced according to a French recipe that dates back to the time of Napoleon III. Like all Prestat products, they are available by mail order. This company has changed ownership and location numerous times, but since the 1980s Prestat has reigned supreme in Princess Arcade, London.

Puyricard
Quartier Beaufort
13090 Puyricard

France
tel (33 42) 21 1326
Run by Marie-Anne and Jean-Guy Roelands, who came from the
Belgian Congo to the Provençal village of Puyricard in 1968.

Ramon Roca Chocolates
Mercaders 6
17004 Gerona
Spain
tel (34 72) 203 662
fax (34 72) 206 337
Founded by the Roca family in 1928. Ramon Roca Vinals, one of the
company's two *maître chocolatiers*, has been working with chocolate for
42 years. The other *maître chocolatier* is Ramon Roca Miralles, who has
had 15 years experience in chocolate making.

Rococo
321 Kings Road
London SW3 5EP
United Kingdom
tel (44 171) 352 5857
Rococo is known not just for its quality products, its London location
and marketing, but also for its founder, Chantal Coady. Chantal has
published books on chocolate and its history and founded the
Chocolate Society of Great Britain. Set amongst fashionable stores
in London's King's Road, Rococo is a chocaholic's dream, filled with
flavoured truffles and hand-dipped chocolates. Try the lavender-
flavoured truffles, or the ones filled with other herb flavourings, tea
flavours or go for the traditional with the exquisite raspberry hand-
dipped truffles.

Rogers Chocolates
913 Government Street
Victoria
British Columbia V8W 1X5
Canada
tel (1 604) 384 7021
fax (1 604) 384 5750
Towards the end of the 19th century, Charles 'Candy' Rogers started
out as a greengrocer who also stocked candies that he imported from

San Francisco. Having discovered that his supply was unreliable, he began producing his own confections, a practice continued by his wife after his death in the late 1920s. The business has since passed through several hands, and while some chocolates are still made at the back of the original store, most are produced at a factory outside Victoria.

Russell Stover Candies
1201 Linwood
Kansas City
MO 64109
United States of America
tel (1 816) 753 8300

You can find boxes of Russell Stover Candies in almost every supermarket, drug store and convenience store throughout Canada and the USA. Established in 1923, this dynamic company has become one of North America's largest chocolate manufacturers over the past 20–30 years. Russell Stover Candies also owns the Whitmans Candy Company — both names are strong throughout the USA and can be found side by side on the shelves.

Sees Candy Shops
PO Box 5027
Rancho Mirage
CA 92270
United States of America
tel (1 619) 340 1505

Today an icon of the American candy industry, Sees was founded by Charles A. See, a pharmacist-turned-confectioner. Noting the success of the Laura Secord company, he moved to California from his native Canada in 1920. With a business partner, James W. Reed, he opened the first Sees Candy Shop at 135 North Western Avenue, using the favourite candy recipes of his mother, Mary.

Charles survived the Depression by cutting the prices of his candies and negotiating lower rents for his stores. He forged ahead with a new factory and developed a quantity order and mail order program. During World War II, the company overcame rationing and the departure of workers (including Charles' own sons) into the armed forces by scaling back production and and reducing store hours, often only to see queues of customers at opening time. Like many old companies, Sees eventually changed hands, but in 1996 the company celebrated its 75th birthday and still powers on today.

Sprungli
Bahnhoffstrasse 21
8022 Zürich
Switzerland
Written enquiries only

A second branch of the original Sprungli family business, which was founded in 1836 by David Sprungli. In 1892, Rudolf Sprungli divided the business between his two sons: Johann, who took over the chocolate factory, now known as Lindt & Sprungli; and David, who continued the confectionery business in Paradeplatz, Zürich.

Teuscher Chocolates of Switzerland
255 Grant Ave.
San Francisco
California
United States of America
Written enquiries only

Thorntons
(various stores in the UK)
(44 1773) 542 493

Found in almost every corner of England and Ireland, Thorntons have been famed for their quality chocolates, especially their Continental range, for decades. With their modern stores and reputation for quality hand-crafted chocolates, Thorntons remains an English icon.

Valhrona
14 Avenue du President Roosevelt
26600 Tain L'Hermitage
France
tel (33 75) 07 90 62

Based south of Paris, Valhrona sells its chocolates through upmarket department stores throughout the world. Valhrona chocolate is renowned for both its distinctive, high-quality packaging and its cocoa strength — reputedly up to 70 per cent. This strength makes it a sought-after chocolate in the chocolate and pastry industries.

Van Houten and Zoon
PO Box 120
Beemdelaan Vaals
The Netherlands
Written enquiries only

The company founded by Coenraad Van Houten, one of the true fathers of the chocolate industry, is today owned by Klaus Jacob, also the owner of the worldwide Barry Callebaut industrial chocolate giant. Van Houten products can be found throughout Europe and quality stores throughout North America and Asia. The most common Van Houten product is cocoa — the foundation product of the company.

E. Wedel S.A.
Zamoyskiege 28–30
03–801 Warszawa
Poland
tel (48 22) 670 7070
fax (48 22) 670 7071
Founded in 1851 by Karol Wedel and eventually named after his son, Emil, whose signature became the company's logo. The name of this Polish chocolate and confectionery company is now recognised by 95 per cent of the Polish population. In 1927, Jan Wedel, grandson of Karol, built the Warsaw factory which is still in use today. E. Wedel received the Grand Prix Award for quality at the Pozan Trade Fair in 1929, and by the 1930s the company owned stores in Poland, Paris and London, with fresh products transported in the company's private aircraft. After World War II, E. Wedel was nationalised by the Communist government, but in 1991 it was re-privatised and listed on the Warsaw stock exchange. Today E. Wedel has approximately 3000 employees and a range of 300 products.

Wittamer
12 Place du Grand Sablon
Grote Zavel 12
1000 Brussels
Belgium
tel (32 2) 512 8451
The world of chocolate would not be complete without the famed Wittamer company. Originally a Belgian patisserie and chocolaterie based in the Belgian antique quarter of Grand Sablon, this company was established in 1910 by Henri Wittamer. Since 1984, Wittamer has had its own confectionery store, which can also be found on Place du Grand Sablon. A must for the chocaholic traveller, Wittamer offers high-grade chocolate with hundreds of fillings and a mouth-watering array of fresh daily concoctions.

Whitmans Candies
PO Box 6070
Philadelphia
PA 19114
United States of America
tel (1 215) 464 6000
Famed for its Whitmans Sampler, a box of chocolates with a distinctive cross-stitch patterned box or tin, Whitmans Candies can be found throughout the United States and Canada. When launched in Australia in 1996 they were an immediate success. Founded in 1842 in Philadelphia by Stephen F. Whitman, the company is today owned by the Russell Stover Candy Corporation.

Other companies to contact:

Altmann & Kuhne
Graben 30
1010 Vienna
Austria
tel (43 1) 533 0927

Angelina
226 Rue de Rivoli
75001 Paris
France
tel (33 1) 4260 8200
fax (33 1) 4344 8235

Available in the USA at:

Chocolat
2039 Bellevue Square
Bellevue
Washington 98004
tel (1800) 808 2462

Andes Chocolate
1400 E. Wisconsin
Delavan
WI 53115
United States of America
Written enquiries only

Anthon Berg Ltd
DK — 2750 Ballerup
Copenhagen
Denmark
Written enquiries only

BCCCA
The Biscuit, Cake, Chocolate
and Confectionery Alliance
37–41 Bedford Row
London WC1R 4JH
United Kingdom
tel (44 171) 404 9111

Charlemagne
8 Place Jacques Brel
4040 Herstal
Belgium
tel (32 41) 64 6644
fax (32 41) 64 4518

Chocolats Klaus S.A.
Ch–2400 Le Locle
Switzerland
Written enquiries only

Christian Constant
26 Rue Du Bac
75007 Paris
France
tel (33 1) 4703 3000

Confectionery Manufacturers of Australasia
PO Box 527
Camberwell
Victoria 3124
Australia
tel (61 3) 9813 1600
fax (61 3) 9882 5473

Duc d'Or
Chocolaterie H.Verhelst N.V.
9150 Kruibeke
Belgium
Written enquiries only

Dudle
Weggisgasse 34
Lucerne CH–6004
Switzerland
tel (41 41) 51 2767
fax (41 41) 51 2764

Elizabeth Shaw Chocolates
Leaf United Kingdom
Greenbank
Bristol BS5 6HR
United Kingdom
Written enquiries only

Ethel M Chocolates Inc
Las Vegas
Nevada 89193
United States of America
tel (1800) 438 4356

Fannie May/Fanny Farmer
Archibald Candy Corp.
1137 West Jackson Boulevard
Chicago
Illinois 60607
United States of America
tel (1 312) 243 2700
fax (1 312) 243 5504

ICAM S.P.A.
22053 Lecco (Como)
Lecco
Italy
tel (39 341) 36 61 32

Jacques Chocolaterie S.A.
Rue de l'industrie 16
B 4700 Eupen
France
tel (33 87) 59 29 11

Joseph Schmidt Confections
3489 16th Street
San Francisco
CA 94114
United States of America
tel (1 415) 861 8682
fax (1 415) 861 3923

Kims Chocolates NV/SA
Industriezone B 615
B–3200 AARSCHOT
Belgium
tel (32 16) 562 143
fax (32 16) 569 242

Konditorei Heinemann
GmbH & Co
Postfach 10 07 21
41007 Monchengladbach
Germany
tel (49 2161) 6930
fax (49 2161) 693 193

La Fontaine au Chocolat
101 & 210 Rue St-Honoré
75001 Paris
France
Written enquiries only

Max Felchlin
Fabrik Fur Die Konditorei
Bahnhofstrasse 63
CH 6430 Schwyz
Switzerland
tel (41 41) 819 6575

Mazet De Mantargis S.A.
B.P.344–45203
Montargis
Cedex
France
tel (33 38) 98 00 29
fax (33 38) 98 25 59

Moonstruck Chocolatier
6663 SW BVTN-Hillsdale Highway
Ste 194
Portland
Oregon 97225
United States of America
Written enquiries only

Pernigotti
Gianduiotto Prodotto DA
Pernigotti S.P.A
Novi Ligure (AL)
Italy
Written enquiries only

Poulain Chocolat Confiserie
B.P.727 41007 Blois Cedex
B 775 598 816
Paris, France
Written enquiries only

Rademaker B.V. (Dutch Cocoa and
Chocolate Company)
Harmenjansweg 129 POB9
Haarlem
The Netherlands
Written enquiries only

Sara Jayne
517 Old York Road
London SW18 1TF
United Kingdom
tel (44 181) 874 8500

Schoko GMBH
Lyoner Str 23
60523 Frankfurt
Germany
Written enquiries only

Terrys Suchard
Bishopthorpe Road
York YO1 1YE
United Kingdom
tel (01904) 653090
fax (01904) 623 434

Torras
CTRA Girona Barcelona KM 15
17844 Cornella de Terra
Girona, Spain
tel (34 972) 581 000

Van Leer Chocolate Corporation
110 Hoboken Avenue
PO Box 2006, Jersey City
New Jersey 07303–2006
United States of America
tel (1 201) 798 8080
fax (1 201) 798 0138

chocolate on the web

Technological change has always influenced the production of chocolate, and the new technology of the Internet is now changing the way that manufacturers and enthusiasts of chocolate promote and discuss the product. The World Wide Web currently features some 3000–5000 chocolate-related sites, including a wealth of recipes to inspire your cooking. Many of these sites, however, merely reproduce information that already exists in books. I have therefore listed, for your browsing pleasure, 18 of the most original and interesting of the current websites. When you have exhausted these, you can always search for the very latest on the subject by entering the magic word CHOCOLATE.

http://www.iic.com/chandre
Discover the SINSATION home chocolate tempering machine.

http://www.GOURMAIL.com
US-based company selling 5 kg (10 lb) whole slabs of Callebaut, Cacao Barry and Nestlé Peters couvertures.

http://m-ms.com
The website for M&Ms, 'the chocolate that melts in your mouth — not in your hand'. The site includes links to an ordering system, complete with a 'Colourworks' machine, allowing you to order your own selection of colours.

http://www.hersheys.com
Includes historical information about Milton Hershey and his company, along with a factory tour and shopping information.

http://www.barcalap.com.sg
A relatively new site from the newly merged Barry Callebaut company. Provides a history of both former companies, their merger, and the company's new college for the study of chocolate making.

http://www.cadbury.co.uk
Everything from a factory tour to a guide to applying for jobs at Cadbury. Not the most modern of sites, but growing by the month.

http://guylian-cho.com
Home of Guylian chocolates of Belgium.

http://www.Ghirardellisq.com
Visit Ghirardelli Square without being buffeted by the wind blowing in from San Francisco Bay. The site offers historical information about Ghirardelli and also profiles some of the products. In case you do decide to visit in person, a map of the square shows the location of all the stores and historical sites.

http://www.godiva.com
Up-market and classy website that tells the history of Godiva and explains how to order the company's products.

http://www.icco.org
This is one of the most informative sites around. The International Cocoa Organisation provides the chocolate-lover with information on cocoa and the cocoa futures market, as well as links to numerous other websites dedicated to chocolate. If you are seeking a place to start, this is it.

http://www.nestle.com
From the home of Nestlé comes this informative website on the products and companies that make up the corporation, as well as a historical portrait of Henri Nestlé and the chance to win books.

http://www.chocibarra.com.mx
A Spanish language site. Ibarra is a renowned brand name in Mexico. The style of the company's chocolates is unique.

http://www.chocolate.co.uk
From the United Kingdom, the home page of the Chocolate Society. There are links to numerous other sites and information is provided on how to become a member.

http://www.lindtchocolate.com
A Lindt and Sprungli site packed with information about this famous Swiss company. A perfect starting point before visiting Switzerland to sample the company's product at the source.

http://www.guittard.com

From the Californian home of Guittard, history and information about the company, one of the big names in US chocolate manufacturing.

http://www.rockychoc.com

The website of the Canadian Rocky Mountain Chocolate Company, offering information on store locations, products and the history of the company.

http://crunchie.co.uk

This site, linked to the Cadbury home page, is dedicated to the Crunchie bar. Historical and fun information about the Crunchie, as well as advertising campaigns designed around this bar.

http://meiji.co.jp

The first name in chocolate in Japan. This site provides information on the Meiji company and its products, which are unknown to many in the West.

my favourite chocolatiers

The following list of stores and factories is a personal assortment, like a selection of favourite chocolates, and is not meant to be comprehensive. While I have mentioned three different Godiva stores, for instance, there are many more. The places on the list are not necessarily even famous, yet in their own special way each has added a little extra romance to the world of chocolate in which I travel.

Bonbon Jeanette
Europaplain 87
1078 GZ Amsterdam
The Netherlands
tel (31 20) 664 9638
fax (31 20) 675 6543
Bonbon Jeanette is a sweet mix of old-style European elegance and marketing bravura. While in recent years the Dutch have not been as well known for their chocolate as their Swiss and Belgian neighbours, Bonbon Jeanette is attempting to change that by supplying chocolate to Belgium, as well as to the rest of the continent. With chocolatier Menno Koerts Meijier masterminding an innovative range of chocolates and gianduja, pastes and pralines, Bonbon Jeanette is set to have a major impact on the European chocolate world.

Cadbury Confectionery
Claremont
Tasmania
Australia
tel (61 3) 6249 0111
As an eight- or nine-year-old child I made my first trip to the Cadbury factory. If only I knew then, as they say, what I know now — although

I travelled to the factory many times in my childhood, the biggest thrill for me was returning to the factory in my early twenties as the official Cadbury Chef.

Tours are conducted almost daily, but it is advisable to phone ahead to make a booking and check scheduling.

Cadbury World
Bournville
Birmingham
B30 2LU
United Kingdom
tel (44 21) 451 4130

As the Vatican is to Catholics and Lords is to cricket fans, the Cadbury factory at Bournville in Birmingham is holy ground for serious chocolate worshippers. While working for Cadbury I made my first pilgrimage to this cathedral of chocolate factories, and from that day on I knew that I was not just working in chocolate for a living, or because the money was good, but also because my life was meant to be devoted to chocolate.

Cadbury World has become a major tourist attraction, and in addition to entertaining school children it provides an interesting day for anyone with even a slight interest in chocolate. The tour covers the company's history as well as its production techniques, and offers complimentary samples along the way. This is fun, fascination and education, all rolled into one.

Cadbury World is open throughout the year, but bookings are advisable, especially in school holidays when only a limited number of tickets are available. There is a charge for the tour, but it is well worth the money, and the cost is compensated for by the low-priced chocolates in the company shop.

Chocolate Heaven
Pier 39
San Francisco
United States of America
Written enquiries only

My sister alerted me to this traveller's haven after her second trip to this great city. Not far from Ghirardelli Square on Pier 39, Chocolate Heaven is a store for the ardent chocaholic. If heaven is all things to all people, so is this store, selling everything from chocolate Band-Aids to CDs that play music on the tongue, as well as more conventional products by Toblerone, Hershey and Lindt.

If you cannot make it to San Francisco yourself, send for the Chocolate Heaven catalogue or ask a friend to pick up a copy for you. True chocaholics always seem to have chocolate winging towards them in the mail.

Chocolatto
1009 Yonge Street
Toronto
Canada
tel (1 416) 922 4011
Chocolatto is a small patisserie/chocolaterie on Toronto's main street, though just outside the city centre. As a pastry chef I have always envied those who run small pastry businesses such as this, where the atmosphere is relaxed yet stylish, and the customers eagerly flock through the doors. The high-quality, modern and sophisticated desserts and pastries (not all of them containing chocolate) are very reasonably priced considering the modest size of the store and the fact that, unlike many establishments, Chocolatto does not attempt to sell day-old stock. Chocolatto is a definite must on any visit to Canada.

D'Anvers Chocolates
PO Box 121
Railton 7305
Tasmania
Australia
tel (03) 6496 1268
Operating entirely out of Tasmania, D'Anvers Chocolates is, in fact, the creation of a Belgian chocolatiere who has relocated to the same Australian state chosen by George Cadbury to establish a factory. D'Anvers is not a particularly old company or a large one, but the quality of its truffles is absolutely exquisite. As with many fine Australian chocolates, I first received a sample of these truffles from my sister on Chocolate Day, 12 August, when we always exchange chocolate gifts that the other has never encountered before. I had certainly never tasted truffles of this quality and flavour. Phone and mail orders are possible from this Belgian chocolatiere whose truffles are so highly regarded that the Belgians themselves are now importing them.

Death By Chocolate
818 Burrard Street (At Robson)
Vancouver
Canada
tel (1 604) 688 8234

Death By Chocolate began in New Zealand in 1991, and since then has become an international franchise with stores in Canada, Australia, New Zealand and Singapore, with many more planned for around the world. The stores have pioneered a new phenomenon: designer desserts — sophisticated and stylish dishes prepared in a Dessert Presentation Area, a stage for the dessert performance. The stores are fun, affordable venues that inform customers and promote chocolate.

Fauchon
26–30 Place de la Madeleine
75008 Paris
France
tel (33 1) 4742 6011

I was introduced to Fauchon by my friend Bob Hart of the *Herald-Sun* newspaper in Melbourne, who warned, 'Don't come back if you don't bring me something from Fauchon.' I had never heard of the place and immediately asked after it when I got to Paris. Despite my poor French, every Parisian was able to direct me to the Fauchon department store, which is renowned for its pastries, fine foods and chocolate. Fauchon is a gourmet's paradise that you will never ever forget. Unfortunately, neither will your wallet.

Fauchon outlets can also be found in other locations around the world, including the Takashimya shopping malls in Singapore and Tokyo.

Godiva
260 Madison Avenue
New York 10016
United States of America
tel (1 212) 951 2888

247 Regent Street
London W1
United Kingdom
tel (44 171) 495 2845

2nd Level Atrium
The Shopping Gallery
Hilton International
Singapore 238883
tel (65) 734 9859
Before I had ever visited their stores, I loved what I had read about Godiva. Today I adore the chocolates and the Godiva concept, which is to present their chocolates in beautiful packaging in stylish and sophisticated stores. In the words of a colleague, however: 'The stores aren't just beautiful to look at. The staff are so knowledgeable about the art of chocolate that it's a pleasure talking to them.'

The London and New York stores are a trip back into a world of elegance, style and true upmarket sophistication, while the Singaporean store is classily modern. On the same second-floor level in the Singapore Hilton, you can also find the Godiva Cafe, where you can enjoy a fine hot chocolate with slices of 'symphony' or 'rhapsody' cakes. If Godiva does not excite the naked envy of its competitors, it ought to, as the standard it sets is so high.

Harrods
87–135 Brompton Road
Knightsbridge
London SW1
United Kingdom
tel (44 171) 730 1234
Harrods is famous for many reasons, and its chocolates, chocolate cakes and pastries should be included among them. The old-world charm of the food halls, especially the chocolate and pastry section, adds to the romance of the food. Try to visit between November and March, as the crush of the crowd in peak season is likely to distract you from the chocolates and pastries. While working in London I once saved for two weeks to buy a chocolate brownie sundae in Harrods.

Island Produce
16 Degraves Street
South Hobart 7004
Tasmania
Australia
tel (61 3) 6223 3233

As a child I loved chocolate in virtually any form, yet I disliked the gritty texture of the chocolate fudge that people served up to me. In early adulthood, however, my sister sent me a small crate of chocolate fudges in four different flavours as a birthday present. Due to my earlier experiences I left it unopened for some time, until eventually, in a chocolate-fix frenzy, I ripped open one of the packages, a jaffa-orange flavoured fudge. The piece was small and vacuum packed, easy to slice and topped with a layer of real chocolate. I remained sceptical until the fudge hit my tongue.

Ever since then I have been addicted to Island Produce fudges. The fudge has become widely known in Australia, and in all my international travels I have never tasted its equal. Mail orders are available, so treat yourself by sending away for boxes of the stuff.

MacRobertsons Factory
346 Jalan Boon Lay
Jurong
Singapore 619528
Written enquiries only

As a chocolate consultant I was fascinated to see the inner workings of this factory, where cocoa beans arrive fresh from plantation drying beds and end up as cocoa butter, cocoa powder and cocoa liquor. The MacRobertsons factory is not open to visitors without special permission, and my tour there is one of the most memorable experiences of my career. As an avid collector of chocolate memorabilia, I have deep and fond memories of MacRobertsons — its products are some of the world's most highly prized collectables.

Panache
33–35 Knightsbridge
London SW1X 7NL
United Kingdom
tel (44 171) 235 8819

Panache has been in business for many years, but I first came upon this delightful store in 1989. At first I failed to realise it was a chocolate shop — I was simply drawn to what was one of the most colourful and impressive shop window displays I had ever seen. Soon I discovered that the store's chocolates were European premium quality. The chocolate orange sticks were divine. As the weeks went by I regularly passed Panache and noticed that the displays took on seasonal and event-based colour schemes, from autumn tones to the lilac of spring, making me aware for the first time of the importance of chocolate shop window dressing. Panache's window displays are still just as colourful, and its chocolates are as good as ever.

Perugina
520 Madison Ave.
New York 10022
United States of America
tel (1 212) 688 2490

Outside of the USA and its original home of Italy, Perugina is not spectacularly well known, although as part of the Nestlé group the company will no doubt raise its international profile. Best known for its Baci ('kisses') chocolates, Perugina has an extensive range of other boxed and packaged chocolates. The Perugina store on Madison Avenue is renowned for its displays of chocolate and packaging, as well as for the quality and flavour of its products, which compare favourably in price to some of the other chocolates on sale in New York. Perugina is on the way uptown to Central Park, so stop on by.

Richart Design et Chocolate
7 East 55th Street
New York 10022
United States of America
tel 1800 RICH-ART

My first encounter with the Richart Design et Chocolate store was purely accidental. Stuck in a taxi in a New York traffic jam, I had decided to trudge the remaining few blocks to my hotel, but I had only walked a few paces when the scent of chocolate wafted past. To my surprise, the store from which this aroma came looked less like a chocolate shop than a gallery of modern art: spare, precise, cold. I was not deterred. Inside I discovered that Richart chocolate is itself a form of modern art.

In reality, Richart is not a cold environment, but a clear and uncluttered space for the display of exceptionally high-quality chocolate. It's expensive, so Richart may remain a store that you visit only once and dream of evermore; yet the desire for chocolate is, after all, a part of its allure — a chase that need not always end in a catch. Richart Design is the perfect place to press your nose against the unattainable. On the other hand, you could always dig deeply for that single chocolate to savour in your memory forever.

glossary

Aerated Chocolate

Aerated chocolate, with its characteristic fine-bubbled texture, is produced using one of three methods: adding fatty substances before whipping; placing tempered chocolate in a vacuum; mixing the chocolate with carbon dioxide under pressure. Well-known bars produced by aeration include Nestlé's Aero Bar and Cadbury's Wispa.

Alkalised Cocoa

See 'Dutching'.

Amelonado

Spanish for 'melon-like'. The amelonado is the most common of the four varieties of cocoa beans used in modern chocolate manufacturing. It is primarily grown in West African countries such as the Ivory Coast and Ghana.

Assortment

Box of milk or plain chocolates (or a combination of both) with a variety of centres.

Bakers' Chocolate

See 'Compound'.

Bitter Chocolate

See 'Unsweetened Chocolate'.

Bittersweet Chocolate

A dark chocolate with a sugar content between that of bitter and semi sweet chocolate. Also known in some countries as semisweet chocolate.

Block Chocolate

The moulded form of chocolate for retail or industrial sale. Blocks of retail chocolate range in size from 50 g (2 oz) to 1 kg (2 lb), while the standard industrial sized block is 5 kg (10 lb).

Bloom

Refers to either fat or sugar bloom on the surface of chocolate. Chocolate melts at 40°C (104°F), causing cocoa butter or sugar to rise to the surface, leaving a white powdery film (fat bloom), or crystallised sugar (sugar bloom). Neither affects the flavour, although they can look unsightly.

Boxed Chocolates

See 'Assortment'.

Bulk Liquid Transportation

The transportation of chocolate in a liquid form, thought to have been devised by the Callebaut family of Belgium. Liquid chocolate is pumped into a transportation tanker at the manufacturing plant then transported to the end user, where it is pumped directly into heated vats or storage silos.

Caraque

A fine shaving or curl of decorative chocolate, usually 10 cm (4 in) or more in length.

Centrepiece

Any large chocolate structure displayed on a cake or in the centre of a table or dessert trolley.

Chocolate

A mixture of cocoa mass or cocoa with one or more sugars, with or without cocoa butter — although cocoa butter is commonly regarded as the ingredient that distinguishes chocolate from compound.

Chocolate Chips

Small droplets of chocolate. Sometimes also refers to roughly chopped chocolate. Used in chocolate chip cookies, ice creams, mousses, etc.

Chocolate Liqueur

Not to be confused with cocoa liquor. Chocolate liqueurs are relatively new products that derive from the well known crème de cacao. Milk and white chocolate liqueurs, made from chocolate, cream and brandy (or similar) are now widely available.

Chocolate Rough

Chocolate thickened with roasted or desiccated coconut. The coconut gives the finished chocolate a roughened texture. Also the name of a retail chocolate product used for decoration.

Chocolate Substitute

See 'Compound'.

Chocolate Vermicelli

Rigid strands of chocolate which are usually broken into small splinters and sprinkled over cakes. Often 'panned' to give the chocolate a glossy shine (see 'Panning').

Cluster

An English version of the traditional Swiss *chocolat rocher*. A cluster is made from whole or chopped almonds, peanuts or other nuts, which are welded with chocolate into a bite-sized conglomerate. In contrast to the *rocher*, the nuts are not flavoured or treated, other than by roasting.

Coating

See 'Compound'. May also refer to chocolate glazes, ganaches, etc.

Cocoa

The powder produced from cocoa press cake, which is the solid portion of the cocoa bean that remains after the extrusion of cocoa butter and liquor. Cocoa powder may subsequently be treated with alkali or alkaline salts (see 'Dutching').

Cocoa Bean

The seed of *Theobroma cacao*, the cocoa tree.

Cocoa Butter

The natural fat derived from the cocoa bean.

Cocoa Liquor

The liquid essence of the cocoa bean, prior to the extraction of cocoa butter. Computerised blending of liquors is used to give some chocolates their distinctive flavours.

Cocoa Mass

The paste produced by the mechanical crushing of cocoa nibs, with a butter content of not less that 480 g per kilogram.

Cocoa Mother

Trees which are grown among cocoa trees to provide shade and protection from the elements.

Cocoa Neat Work

See 'Cocoa Mass'.

Cocoa Nib

The roasted cocoa bean freed from its shell or husk, with or without the germ.

Cocoa Painting

The art of applying solutions of cocoa powder mixed with liquid, usually alcohol, onto a 'canvas' of pastillage (hardened icing (confectioners') sugar paste). Different tones are produced with stronger or weaker solutions. Used extensively by top pastry chefs from the 17th to the early part of the 19th century, cocoa painting is still practised today in large hotels and banquet facilities, where the pastry chef has time to impress.

Cocoa Powder

See 'Cocoa'.

Cocoa Press Cake

See 'Cocoa'.

Cocoa Solids

The dry residue of cocoa mass. Also produced with the fat content removed.

Collar

A girdle of chocolate wrapped around a cake for decorative purposes, or to contain a topping of cream, crème, mousse or fruit.

Coloured Chocolate

White chocolate with food-standard colouring added. Chocolate colouring must be oil- rather than water-based, as water damages the structure of chocolate. Coloured chocolate may be used in flood work or in decorations for cakes or desserts.

Compound

Compound is a variety of chocolate in which the cocoa mass and butter have been replaced by cocoa powder and vegetable fat. As a result, compound has an inferior flavour, yet it has the advantage of not requiring tempering. It is therefore ideal for dipping, decorations and writing messages. Also referred to as coating, melt, dipping, or bakers' chocolate (not to be confused with the US brand of the same name).

Conching

The process of heating and stirring chocolate paste and cocoa butter in large troughs or basins, called conche machines (derived from the Spanish word 'concha', meaning 'shell'). Heavy metal or granite rollers swirl through the mixture for up to 72 hours, giving it a velvety smoothness. Conching increases the caramelisation of milk chocolate and enriches the flavour of dark chocolate.

Conditioning

The protection of moulded chocolate from humidity or heat.

Cooking Chocolate

A cheaper product than eating chocolate on account of a lower cocoa butter content, which is nevertheless sufficient to give a fuller chocolate flavour than that produced by cocoa powder or compound.

Count Line

Any variety of confection, usually wrapped individually, which is sold by number rather than weight.

Couverture

The highest grade of pure chocolate, containing 45 per cent or more cocoa butter.

Crack

The term describing the snapping sound of well-finished chocolate. A good crack indicates successful tempering and conditioning.

Criollo

'Native'. The name of one of the four major varieties of cocoa bean. The fresh criollo bean is almost white inside and does not require prolonged fermentation. Criollo produces a pale, delicately flavoured chocolate, which dominated the world market until the mid-18th century then fell rapidly out of favour.

Crumb

The coarse powder produced from a dried mixture of whole milk, sugar and cocoa liquor.

Curl

An elaborate form of chocolate shaving, created from a strip of half-set chocolate, rather than carved from a block. Curls come in several styles: white, milk, dark, marbled (a mixture of the three different varieties), and two-tone (a combination of any two).

Dark Chocolate

See 'Unsweetened Chocolate'.

Dipping Chocolate

See 'Compound'.

Dots

See also 'Chocolate Chips'. A smaller version of chocolate chips, usually produced on a steel band machine.

Drinking Chocolate

A mixture of cocoa mass or cocoa with one or more sugars, with or without cocoa butter. Drinking chocolate must be water-free and contain a minimum of 150 g of non-fat cocoa solids per kilogram.

Dutching

The process of cocoa alkalisation, designed to alter cocoa's colour by adding chemicals such as potassium carbonate. Natural cocoa has a pH level (measuring acidity/alkalinity) of 5.0 to 5.5; dutching usually increases the pH of the cocoa to between 7.0 and 7.5, although heavily alkalised cocoa, which is almost black in colour, has a pH of 9.0. Also known as the 'Dutch process'.

Easter Eggs

The generic term for all egg-shaped chocolates sold for the celebration of Easter. The egg is originally thought to have been a pagan fertility symbol, associated with springtime in the northern hemisphere, though the breaking of Easter eggs is also regarded by some Christians as a symbol of Christ's resurrection from the cave in which his body is said to have been laid after crucifixion. In the past it was common for Easter eggs to contain small gifts, whose 'freeing' represented the resurrection. Easter eggs are commonly thought to be made from 'special' chocolate, but this is not the case — all varieties of chocolate are used in their production.

Eating Chocolate

Any pure chocolate intended for eating.

Enrobing

The process of encasing any centre, praline or filling in a coating of chocolate.

Faux Bois

A French phrase which literally means 'false wood'. Refers to a method of creating patterns on chocolate resembling the grain of wood. This is done by pouring liquid chocolate onto plastic sheets or non-stick parchment paper and imprinting it with a curved rubber 'stamp'. The rubber is patterned with semi-circular grooves which can be dragged over the chocolate or rocked back and forth. The imprinted chocolate may be used as a collar for a cake, or left to set before being covered with a thin layer of a different coloured chocolate. The finished product can then be cut into pieces.

Fermenting

The process of placing beans from freshly-picked cocoa pods under branches or banana leaves for between two and six days. This removes unwanted pulp, destroys the beans' germination properties, eradicates bitterness and triggers the development of a cocoa flavour.

Filigree

A freehand piped-chocolate decoration for cakes, pastries, desserts, etc. Usually very fine in design. May take the form of a structured pattern, or a 'drizzled' web of chocolate that is subsequently broken into decorative fragments.

Flake

See 'Rolling'.

Flavoured Chocolate

Any chocolate containing oil-based flavours or essences. Orange, lemon, strawberry and raspberry are just some of the many flavours available. Appropriate colouring is sometimes added to flavoured chocolate, making it useful for mousses, decorations, etc. Chocolate flavoured for professional purposes rarely contains fruit pieces, which are more commonly found in retail chocolate.

Flood Work

Originally a technique used to decorate wedding cakes with royal icing, now winning favour among chocolate enthusiasts. Place a decoration design under non-stick baking parchment paper, which is translucent, and trace the outline with dark chocolate squeezed from a thin-tipped paper piping bag. When the outline has set, fill in the gaps with a different coloured chocolate, once again using the bag. Allow to set firmly then peel from the paper. With a little practice, you can augment the natural white, milk and dark chocolate colours with coloured white chocolate (see 'Coloured Chocolate'), creating amazing effects resembling animation.

Fondante

A type of chocolate, created by Lindt of Switzerland, with a fine texture reminiscent of fondant.

Forastero

A Spanish term meaning 'foreign', describing one of the main varieties of cocoa beans used in chocolate manufacturing.

Grinding

The stage during chocolate production in which crushed and blended beans are ground and heated into a thick paste known as cocoa mass, 55 per cent of which is cocoa butter.

Leaf

A decoration formed by painting or spreading liquid chocolate onto a leaf (usually a rose leaf), which is peeled away when the chocolate has set.

Les Grand Crus

A term created as recently as 1986 by the French Chocolate company Valhrona. Refers to any chocolate made from cocoa beans from a single source. First applied to the company's Guanaja plain couverture, which uses only South American beans, but there are now several styles of Grand Crus. Like many chocolate terms, however, this one has been distorted by companies producing chocolate that does not conform to the original definition. It is therefore worth trying to check whether the term is used accurately on the packaging of any chocolate that you are considering buying.

Melt

See 'Compound'. Also a brand name in some countries.

Milk Chocolate

A product produced with milk solids, containing not less than 45 g per kilogram of milk fat.

Moulding

Not to be confused with the modelling of chocolate. Refers to the process of shaping by pouring the chocolate into a mould made of plastic, silicon or rubber, then allowing to set. The most common moulds available for the home cook are made of cheap plastic for one-off or limited use, or more expensive silicon versions for repeated use. Always wash a mould in warm water with a soft cloth immediately after use. Avoid abrasive washing materials or detergents. Dry the mould with tissue or absorbent paper, and polish the inside with cotton wool. Store clean moulds in a cool area away from direct sunlight, and always clean with cotton wool before using again.

Modelling Chocolate

A mixture made by adding glucose syrup, corn syrup or honey to white, milk or dark chocolate, creating a paste which is firm enough to model into the shapes of flowers, animals, etc. Modelling chocolate can also be rolled into smooth coatings or decorative collars for cakes.

Panning

A technique for coating round candies or scorched nuts, referred to informally as the Volvo process on account of the 'protective' layers of chocolate which are applied. As the name suggests, panning requires a large pan, made of copper, in which the nuts or candies are placed. As the pan is shaken, melted chocolate is applied in hand scoops or a fine spray, then cooled with a jet of air. This process is repeated until the centres are layered with chocolate — manufacturers aim to produce a coating of a similar thickness to the centre.

Piping

The creation of decorations by applying melted chocolate with a piping bag onto baking parchment paper, or directly onto the cake, etc. Depending on the quantity of chocolate being used, you can add one or two drops of glycerine to slightly thicken the chocolate, giving it a finer line. Droplets of water can be used for the same purpose, but this has to carefully controlled. Spoon a small amount of the chocolate into a paper piping (pastry) bag, ensuring that the mixture contains no lumps. Fold the end of the bag. Practise designs on parchment if you intend to work directly onto the cake, or alternatively, do the piping on the parchment then peel away the paper and place the completed design on the cake.

Pure Chocolate

Chocolate that contains only pure cocoa butter.

Roasting

The process of cooking cocoa beans in large ovens to evaporate water, develop aroma and prepare the bean for shelling.

Rolling

The crushing of granular chocolate paste between a series of metal cylinders, giving the chocolate its delicate consistency. Produces a powdery substance known as flake.

Rosette

Any decorative, shaped chocolate product.

Seasonal Lines

Products which are manufactured and sold to meet seasonal demands, such as those that occur before Christmas and Easter.

Seeding

A form of tempering in which the mixture is initially cooled by adding a further two-thirds of chocolate in chopped or shaved form. When the mixture has thickened it is reheated to 32°C (90°F).

Shelf Lines

Identical chocolate sweets which are boxed or packaged for retail sale.

Semisweet Chocolate

A North American term to describe chocolate produced by combining chocolate liquor, cocoa butter and sugar. Commonly used to produce chocolate chips, but also some bars.

Shavings

Shaved fragments of chocolate, usually used to coat truffles or cakes. Approximately 250 g (8 oz) of milk, white or dark (plain or semisweet) chocolate will make enough shavings to cover a 23 cm (9 in) cake. Simply shave a block of chocolate with a vegetable peeler.

Shelling

After roasting, the process by which the shells of cocoa beans are crushed to remove the nib.

Squares

Flat squares produced by slicing chocolate which has been spread thinly onto non-stick baking parchment paper.

Steel Band

A large conveyor belt which circulates chocolates through a cooling tunnel or chamber, causing them to set. Produces confections such as Hershey Kisses and Cadbury Chocolate Buttons.

Sweet Chocolate

Similar to semisweet chocolate, with added sugar.

Tabliering or Tableing

A form of tempering in which cooling takes place by paletting one-third of the molten chocolate onto a marble slab until it cools and thickens, then reintroducing it to the remaining chocolate and reheated to 32°C (90°F).

Tempering

The technique of evenly distributing cocoa butter throughout melted chocolate. This leads to the correct crystallisation of fats, ensuring an attractive gloss and crack.

Thins

Thin squares of chocolate which are usually flavoured or coloured, or both. Occasionally the term refers to a manufactured product consisting of a fine layer of fondant 'enrobed' in chocolate. Mint and orange thins are the most common flavours, and while they are intended as snacks or petit fours, they also make very good decorations for cakes.

Trinitaro

A hybrid of the criollo and forastero cocoa beans.

Unsweetened Chocolate

Also known as 'bitter', 'dark', or 'au naturel', this is pure chocolate liquor, the 'meat' of the cocoa bean, with no added sugar. It has an intense chocolate flavour because of the concentration of cocoa solids. Ranges in taste from sweet to bitter, and is also known as plain, semisweet or sweet chocolate. The most natural of all chocolates.

White Chocolate

Chocolate produced with not less than 200 g of cocoa butter per kilogram, 35 g of milk fat per kilogram, and 105 g of milk solids (non fat) per kilogram.

Winnowing

The use of air jets to separate crushed cocoa shells from the nibs. The chemical industry extracts theobromine (a nerve stimulant and diuretic, similar to caffeine) from a portion of the winnowed cocoa shells. The remainder goes into stock feed.

Wood Effect

See 'Faux Bois'.

Xocolatl

The Aztec term for the drink produced by mixing cocoa beans, spices and water. A combination of the word for 'herb' (xoco) and the word for 'water' (latl).

acknowledgments

I would like to thank the following people and companies for their assistance and generosity in supplying products, information and copious research material from around the world. The position in which these names and companies appears in this list does not refer to their importance or the measure of their generosity. I would like to thank them equally for participating in this project.

David Johnston, Managing Director, Godiva Europe, Brussels; Karin Weissenbach, Head of Operations, PRESTAT, England; Stephen J. Blommer, Marketing Manager, Blommer Chocolate Company, USA; Dana Taylor Davenport, President, Dilettante Chocolates, USA; Jim Conlan, Marketing, M&M/Mars, USA; Gary Willis, National Sales, and Max Pridmore, President, DELMAR International, Australia; John and David Grisold, Chocolatier (Australia) Ltd; Erna Koprax, Marketing Director, Hotel Sacher Wien, Vienna; Jackie Piche, Marketing, Van Leer Chocolate Corporation, USA; Ramon Roca, Ramon Roca Chocolates, Italy; Lucio Q. Leonelli, Managing Director, Baratti and Milano, Italy; Lynne Chambers, Consumer Services Manager, Terry's Suchard, UK; H. Byma, Red Band Venco B.V., Netherlands; John E. Newman OBE, Biscuit, Cake Chocolate and Confectionery Alliance, England; Heinz-Richard Heinemann, Konditorei Heinemann GmbH & Co, Germany; Susanne S. Korsholm, Product Manager, Toms Chocolate, Denmark; Kerry Hudson, Cadbury Schweppes, Australia; Grace T. Leong for Baker's Chocolate Company, Hunter and Associates Inc. Public Relations, USA; Joyce Kempton, Marketing Specialist, Archibald Candy Corp., USA; David N. Fell, Cadbury Food Services, Australia; Marek Andrzej Matysek, Communications Manager, E. Wedel, Poland; Terry Henshaw, Retail Operations Manager, Rogers Chocolates, Canada; G. Corrodi, Public Relations Manager, Lindt and Sprungli, Switzerland; Bernard J. Duclos, ECM, Inc. / Valrhona Chocolate; A. Roulet, Chocolats Camille Bloch SA, Switzerland; Mark T. Haley, President and CEO, Brown and Haley, USA; Robert J. Ingles, Director of Operations,

Chocolaterie Bernard Callebaut, Canada; Benoit Digeon, President, Mazet de Mantargis SA, France; Cecile Wren, Customer Service Representative, Laura Secord, Canada; Robert J. Noxon, Director of Marketing, Ferrero Canada Ltd; Michelle Drysdale, Customer Service Representative, Nestle Canada; Marlene M. Machut, External Relations Manager, M&M/Mars, USA; Neil McIntosh, Marketing Manager, Bendicks of Mayfair, England; Alister and Simon Haigh, Haigh's Chocolates, Australia; Joseph Schmidt, Joseph Schmidt Confections, USA; P. Westerlain, President, Côte de France Chocolatier, France; Jessie Heyndrickx, Assistant Marketing, Guylian Chocolate Company, Belgium; Karin Schilling, Export, DreiMeister; Thierry Schamp, Sales Manager, Le Chocolatier Bruyerre, Brussels; P. Petitjean, Managing Director, Jacques Chocolaterie; Franz Callebaut, General Manager, Callebaut Asia Pacific, Singapore; Luc Moons, Sales and Marketing Manager, Kims Chocolates N.V., Belgium; Anthony Charlton, Director, Ackermans Chocolates, London; William G. Simmons, President, Moonstruck Chocolatier, USA; Andrea Schurpf, Max Felchlin Inc., Switzerland; Sees Candies, USA; ICAM Societa Per Azioni, Italy; Guittard Chocolate Company, USA; Ortrud Munch Carstens, New York, USA; Phillip Bell-Booth, Death By Chocolate Franchise Limited, New Zealand; and Andrea Turner, for all her typing, patience and understanding during the late nights of research and for the months of consuming chocolate on behalf of a greater need.

And a special thanks to the people I have met at demonstrations, lectures and tutorials, and through the course of my career, who have shown such interest in the product that we all have in common, the product that has inspired me to compile this book.

sources

In compiling this book, I was helped by every person mentioned in the acknowledgments. I could not have written it without the assistance of these men and women from the varying companies they represent.

Books that greatly helped me in my research were: *The Dilettante Book of Chocolate and Confections,* by Dana Taylor Devonport; *Cocoa,* Fourth Edition, by G.A.R. Wood, Longman; *Chocolate, Cocoa, and Confectionery, Science and Technology*, Third Edition, by Bernard W. Minnifie, Chapman and Hall; *Family Circle's All About Chocolate*, Murdoch Books, Sydney, 1995; *Chocologie*, Union des Fabricants Suisses de Chocolat, Bern; and *Chocolatier Magazine*, New York.

Other books by Aaron Maree

Aaron Maree's Classic Desserts, Angus & Robertson, Sydney, 1995.
Biscuits, Pastries and Cookies of the World, Angus & Robertson, Sydney, 1992.
Cakes, Tortes and Gâteaux of the World, Angus & Robertson, Sydney, 1991.
Chocolate Cookery with Aaron Maree, Bay Books, Sydney, 1995.
Cookies, Biscuits and Slices of the World, Angus & Robertson, Sydney, 1992.
Patisserie, Angus & Robertson, Sydney, 1995.
Sweet Health, Angus & Robertson, Sydney, 1995.

index
of recipes